SCC

S0-BJH-900

At Issue

Divorce and Children

Other Books in the At Issue Series:

At Issue

| Divorce and Children

Roman Espejo, Book Editor

GREENHAVEN PRESS
A part of Gale, Cengage Learning

GALE
CENGAGE Learning·

Farmington Hills, Mich • San Francisco • New York • Waterville, Maine
Meriden, Conn • Mason, Ohio • Chicago

Patricia Coryell, *Vice President & Publisher, New Products & GVRL*
Douglas Dentino, *Manager, New Products*
Judy Galens, *Acquisitions Editor*

© 2015 Greenhaven Press, a part of Gale, Cengage Learning.

WCN: 01-100-101

Gale and Greenhaven Press are registered trademarks used herein under license.

For more information, contact:
Greenhaven Press
27500 Drake Rd.
Farmington Hills, MI 48331-3535
Or you can visit our Internet site at gale.cengage.com

For product information and technology assistance, contact us at

Gale Customer Support, 1-800-877-4253
For permission to use material from this text or product, submit all requests online at www.cengage.com/permissions.

Further permissions questions can be e-mailed to permissionrequest@cengage.com.

Articles in Greenhaven Press anthologies are often edited for length to meet page requirements. In addition, original titles of these works are changed to clearly present the main thesis and to explicitly indicate the author's opinion. Every effort is made to ensure that Greenhaven Press accurately reflects the original intent of the authors. Every effort has been made to trace the owners of copyrighted material.

Cover photograph copyright © Images.com/Corbis.

LIBRARY OF CONGRESS CATALOGING-IN-PUBLICATION DATA

Divorce and children / Roman Espejo, book editor.
     pages cm. -- (At issue)
     Includes bibliographical references and index.
     ISBN 978-0-7377-7161-9 (hardcover) -- ISBN 978-0-7377-7162-6 (pbk.)
     1. Divorce. 2. Children of divorced parents. I. Espejo, Roman, 1977-
     HQ814.D622 2015
     306.89--dc23
                                                                    2014042429

Printed in Mexico
1 2 3 4 5 6 7 19 18 17 16 15

Contents

Introduction

In some divorces, parents are not the only ones to separate. In families with siblings, for example, one or more of the siblings may primarily live with their mother, while the other sibling or siblings may primarily live with their father. Such a divorce arrangement is known as split custody, which is seldom granted by judges. "Courts in most states are opposed to separating siblings when their parents divorce. Children are experiencing the trauma of their parents' separation, and judges often see parting them from each other as an added cruelty at an already vulnerable time,"[1] states Beverly Bird, a writer with over two decades of experience in family law. Nonetheless, Bird explains, it is pursued when the arrangement is decided to be in the best interest of the separated family. "This doesn't mean, however, that no judge will ever order such an arrangement. It just means that parents have the burden of convincing the court that such divided custody is good for their kids and appropriate to their family's situation."[2]

Bird describes the main factors in which a court may decide for split custody in divorce arrangements. She explains that the parents or children themselves usually request it. "If a child wants to live with one parent, but his sibling wants to live with the other, the judge might acquiesce and approve such an arrangement," she maintains. Another factor Bird cites is economic; child support does not always help a parent adequately provide for all of the children. "In such situations, the children might fare better if each parent's budget is stretching only enough to support one or two of them and their daily needs," she contends. Of course, with split custody comes

1. Beverly Bird, "Separating Siblings with Divorce," LegalZoom, accessed September 21, 2014. http://info.legalzoom.com/separating-siblings-divorce-24316.html.
2. Ibid.

added considerations for the court in deciding divorce arrangements, especially regarding the children's relationships with each other. "They must not only address parents' time with their children, but siblings' time with each other as well. Courts in several states have acknowledged that visitation terms for separated siblings can and should be incorporated into divorce parenting plans,"[3] insists Bird.

Indeed, numerous experts believe that split custody is far from ideal and hurts the relationships between siblings—as well as their emotional, social, and psychological development. For instance, Meriwether & Tharp, a law firm based in Atlanta, Georgia, offers a scenario wherein twin boys—who become even closer because of their mother and father's divorce—are separated in such an arrangement. "There is almost no question that it is healthy for siblings to have a positive relationship with each other. In fact, studies have shown that siblings that enjoy healthy relationships with each other exhibit greater emotional understanding, greater cognitive abilities, greater social understanding, greater moral sensibility, and better psychological adjustment,"[4] the firm states. "Although it is not impossible for siblings being raised in a split parenting arrangement to maintain a strong and nurturing relationship with each other, just as with any other relationship, time and distance can have a negative impact."[5]

Nonetheless, others contend that split custody can benefit children and disagree with the opposition of courts to grant it. Gregory S. Forman, a family law attorney and certified family court mediator, believes the term itself is misunderstood. "Part of the barrier to split custody may be the terminology. Not all 'split custody' situations need to involve one or more children living primarily with one parent and one or

---

3. Ibid.
4. "Is Split Parenting Arrangements Harmful to Children?," *Meriwether & Tharp Divorce Attorney Blog*, November 11, 2013. http://mtlawoffice.com/blog/is-split-parenting -arrangements-harmful-to-children/#sthash.GHk6ppOX.dpuf.
5. Ibid.

more children living primarily with the other,"[6] he writes on his blog. "Often split custody means visitation schedules that have the children spending time apart from each other so that each parent gets individual time with each child." Forman reasons that this is beneficial because it enables parents to bond with a child in ways that his or her siblings may not want to partake in. "Rather than forcing all the siblings to engage in activities that they do not all enjoy or preventing a child from ever getting to do activities he or she enjoys because the siblings don't enjoy them (or because they are not age-appropriate for all the siblings), such a visitation schedule allows both parents to spend some time focusing on an individual child's interests,"[7] he insists.

While uncommon, split custody is just one of the profound ways divorce impacts children. From the painful process of breaking up the family to the long-term effects, the dissolution of a marriage is often viewed as affecting children just as much—and even more—than adults. "There is no such thing as an intelligent divorce,"[8] argues Jann Gumbiner, a psychologist and clinical professor at the University of California, Irvine College of Medicine. "There are no firm rules about a good divorce or a bad divorce. Divorce hurts children, even grown ones."[9]

At Issue: Divorce and Children investigates the issue of divorce from a variety of perspectives, focusing especially on the impact of divorce on children. The viewpoints included investigate such questions as whether divorce is really harmful to children, how divorce affects older children, how it affects kids

---

6. Gregory S. Forman, "What's So Bad About Split Custody?," gregoryforman.com, January 24, 2013. http://www.gregoryforman.com/blog/2013/01/whats-so-bad-about-split -custody.

7. Ibid.

8. Jann Gumbiner, "Divorce Hurts Children, Even Grown Ones," *Psychology Today*, October 31, 2011. http://www.psychologytoday.com/blog/the-teenage-mind/201110 /divorce-hurts-children-even-grown-ones.

9. Ibid.

with special needs, and what steps parents can take to help their children better cope with divorce.

Most Children Adjust to the Negative Effects of Divorce

Sarah-Marie Hopf

Sarah-Marie Hopf is a project strategist fellow at the consulting firm 17 Triggers, in Phnom Penh, Cambodia.

Children are exposed to stressful risks and events when parents divorce, including high conflict, lost relationships, and remarriage, which can result in the development of externalizing or internalizing disorders. Nonetheless, the majority of researchers agree that most children possess the resilience to cope with the stresses and new circumstances of divorce and mature into well-adjusted adults. Along with their temperament and coping skills, as well as age, gender, preexisting mental problems, and other factors, resilient children receive good parenting and have supportive school and social environments. Research on divorce should focus on resilience in children of divorce from a range of cultural, ethnic, and socioeconomic backgrounds to help create intervention programs designed for the needs of diverse families.

Today over 45 percent of marriages in the United States end in divorce and "about 40 percent of children will experience their parents' divorce, with about 80 percent of them placed primarily in the physical custody of their biological mother". Divorce represents one of the most stressful life events for both children and their parents. Major stressors and risk factors include the initial period after separation, parental conflict, the loss of vital relationships, financial problems, and repartnering or remarriage. Many educators, politicians, mental health workers, family theorists, and the media portray divorced families as unfit for the successful upbringing of children. They believe that only married families can provide a warm and nurturing environment in which children can thrive. Some family scholars even argue that "the breakdown of the traditional family [destroys] the basic fabric of American society and contributes to a vast array of social problems that will carry on into future generations".

A few major longitudinal studies such as the [Judith S.] Wallerstein et al. study have supported strong negative effects on children from divorced families. However, one cannot generalize from these studies, because they often used non-representative samples such as clinical samples with pre-existing psychological problems and failed to employ standardized measures to produce reliable and valid data. Therefore, one needs to examine critically the findings of divorce studies. On average, children in married families fare better than children from divorced families. Nevertheless, the vast majority of children possess great resilience and the ability to "cope with or even benefit from their new life situation". Internal factors such as the child's psychological and physical characteristics and external factors such as the immediate and extended family and the community environment influence a child's resilience and ability to cope with parental divorce. Good parenting and extra-familial protective factors such as peer relationships, schools, and support from nonparental adults including mentors and neighbors also contribute to children's resilience and effective coping.

Resilience in children has been studied since the 1960s and 1970s as researchers started to look at human strengths rather than shortcomings and dysfunctions. Although resilience proves difficult to define, it generally refers to "patterns of positive adaptation during or following significant adversity or risk" that allow individuals to "bounce back" to their previous level of well-being or even to attain a higher level of functioning. In the past, much controversy surrounded the study of resilience due to the difficulties associated with "translating definitions into operation in research". Researchers often failed to examine differences in resilience associated with cultural and ethnic backgrounds. Now, researchers are moving towards more standardized measures to obtain greater validity and reliability of their data. Resilience research focuses on assessing risk factors such as stressful life events and protective factors such as the child's personal qualities and environmental interactions such as positive family relationships. Protective factors "moderate the effect of one or more risk factors".

The departure of one parent and inadequate information about the reasons for divorce often cause externalizing disorders and to a lesser degree internalizing disorders in children.

Stressors of the Divorce Process and Adjustment of Children

The effects of divorce-related stressors vary greatly among children and over time. The nature of the initial separation, parental conflict, the loss of vital relationships, financial problems, and repartnering or remarriage of one or both parents play a crucial role in how these stressors affect children's adjustment in the short and long run. Many children express some form of externalizing or internalizing disorders. Externalizing disorders include "antisocial, aggressive, noncompliant behavior and lack of self-regulation, low social responsibility, and diminished cognitive agency and achievement" whereas "anxiety, depressive symptoms and problems with social relationships" represent common internalizing disorders. Further, children from divorced families have a much higher chance of experiencing lower academic performance, dropping out of school, having a teenage pregnancy, and abusing alcohol or drugs than children from married families.

Stress of the Initial Separation

Most children show strong reactions to their parents' divorce, especially over a period of one or two years following divorce. The departure of one parent and inadequate information about the reasons for divorce often cause externalizing disorders and to a lesser degree internalizing disorders in children. Survey studies using such measures as clinical cutoff scores on the Child Behavior Checklist found that about 20–25 percent of children in divorced families, compared to 10 percent of children in non-divorced families, demonstrate severe emotional and behavioral problems.

Custodial mothers often experience a significant reduction in their economic resources after divorce.

Parental Conflict

Many divorce researchers have wondered whether parents should stay together for the sake of their children despite a high-conflict marriage. Divorce represents the better option if it can lessen the amount of conflict and negativity in the children's environment. Conflict between parents during and following separation and divorce represents a major stressor for children and can lead to difficulties in these children's adjustment. Between 20 and 25 percent of children experience high conflict during the marriage of their parents. Some families are able to reduce conflict whereas others continue to fight after divorce. High conflict that involves the child, "conflict that is physically violent, threatening or abusive, and conflict in which the child feels caught in the middle has the most adverse consequences for the well-being of children". In addition, mothers and fathers involved in high conflict marriages often practice poor parenting, because they use harsher discipline and express reduced warmth towards their children. Parents also have to cope with emotional problems resulting from the divorce and therefore take less time to support their children through effective parenting. Some children become the only emotional support of their parents, which puts additional stress on children's shoulders.

Loss of Vital Relationships

Children also have a higher risk of losing significant relationships with friends, family members, and especially the nonresident parent, usually the father. Children's relationships with their fathers frequently deteriorate, because they see each other less frequently. "Between 18 and 25 percent of children have no contact with their fathers 2–3 years after divorce". Many factors such as restricted visitation times, interfering mothers, geographical constraints after moving, psychological problems in fathers and new paternal relationships and remarriage contribute to the diminished relationships between children and their fathers. Boys especially need a close relationship with their fathers and react more strongly to deprivation of paternal contact. Some children purposefully limit the relationships with their fathers if they have abusive or violent tendencies or if the fathers have significant psychological problems and disorders. These decisions represent a healthy choice for the children and protect them from further harm.

Financial Situation

Custodial mothers often experience a significant reduction in their economic resources after divorce, "retaining only about 50–75 percent of their pre-divorce income [as] compared to the 90 percent retained by noncustodial fathers". The effects of income usually affect the families indirectly. For example, they often lead single families to move to less expensive neighborhoods with weaker schools, higher crime rates and less desirable peer groups. Financial support from noncustodial fathers can protect children from these potentially harmful influences and lead to more positive relationships with their children. Paternal custody usually offers better financial support for children. Yet, studies found few differences in the adjustment between mother or father custody arrangements. Nevertheless, some studies suggest that boys do better when in paternal custody. These fathers, representing less than 20 percent of custodial parents, usually take exceptional interest in their children's lives.

Many internal factors such as age, gender, temperament and physical characteristics influence children's resilience to the negative effects of divorce.

Remarriage and Re-partnering

Studies suggest that one third of children will live in a remarried or cohabitating family before the age of 18. Children often experience significant stress when their parents begin a new relationship, especially soon after the divorce and when these children are in early adolescence. The absence of biological ties and the resistance of children make the formation of strong relationships between stepparents and children difficult. The biggest problems arise in complex family structures with children from multiple different parents and stepchildren.

Resilience in Children

Despite the significant stressors associated with divorce, approximately 75–80 percent of children develop into well-adjusted adults with no lasting psychological or behavioral problems. They achieve their education and career goals and have the ability to build close relationships. One study by

[Paul R.] Amato even estimated that "42 percent of young adults from divorced families" received higher well-being scores as compared to young adults from nondivorced families. Therefore, the hardship and pain associated with their parents' divorce made them stronger individuals. Children from high conflict families oftentimes benefit the most from the divorce of their parents as it represents an opportunity for a better life.

Protective Factors Reducing Risk for Children of Divorce

Many internal factors such as age, gender, temperament and physical characteristics influence children's resilience to the negative effects of divorce. Studies have shown that intrafamilial protective factors such as authoritative parenting, children's residence in maternal or paternal custody homes, involvement of noncustodial parents, effective joint-custody arrangements, and involvement of supportive stepparents can significantly reduce the children's risk of developing externalizing or internalizing behaviors. Furthermore, extrafamilial factors such as relationships with peers and nonparental adults, authoritative schools, and interventions such as educational programs for divorced parents to improve parenting or youth groups can also help ease the transition and adjustment of children to their new life situation.

Internal Factors

The influence of a child's age on his or her ability to cope with the stresses of divorce remains largely unclear. Many scholars think that younger children might face a higher risk of negative effects, because they cannot comprehend the causes of the divorce and have fewer resources from which to seek help outside the family environment. On the other hand, older children can often find respite in activities such as sports or hobbies. They can also get help from mentors, teachers

SPRING CREEK CAMPUS

and/or coaches. Studies have found that remarriage especially troubles early adolescents when they have lived in a single-parent home for a long time.

Parenting plays the most important role in the adjustment of children and in the development of externalizing or internalizing behaviors.

Most early research studies reported greater adjustment for girls than for boys. New studies have come to the conclusion that gender differences remain slight. In recent years, greater father involvement and joint custody arrangements have diminished the negative effects on boys who usually benefit from having a father figure in their lives. Both female and male adolescents seem to exhibit higher externalizing and internalizing behaviors as compared to adolescents in nondivorced families. Girls tend to express greater reluctance to their parents' remarriage than boys. Strikingly, "some girls in divorced, mother-headed households emerge as exceptionally resilient individuals, enhanced by confronting challenges and responsibilities that follow divorce when they have the support of a competent, caring adult". These findings do not prove true for boys in mother-, father- or joint-custody arrangements.

Divorce has the most significant negative effects on children with pre-existing psychological and behavioral problems. Children who possess intelligence, competence, self-confidence, and a good sense of humor usually adapt well to any kind of adversity. In addition, an easy temperament and physical attractiveness also prove beneficial. These children often receive more help from others. In general, "the psychologically rich may get richer and the poor get poorer in dealing with the challenges of divorce". In addition, the "steeling or inoculation effect occurs when children's controlled exposure and successful adaptation to current stressors enhances their ability to cope with later stressors". Other areas studied in positive psychology such as self-efficacy and an internal locus of control may also contribute to better coping styles in children.

External Factors

According to the socialization theory, parenting plays the most important role in the adjustment of children and in the development of externalizing or internalizing behaviors. Unfortunately, good parenting usually declines and becomes less authoritative in the initial phase after divorce or remarriage, because parents have to use their energy to adjust to their new circumstances. Children often experience parenting marked by more control, less affection, and reduced communication. Remarriage tends to foster better parenting practices in the custodial parent, whereas parenting in single, divorced families remains more problematic. Studies show that "authoritative parents who are warm, supportive, communicative, and responsive to their children's needs, and who exert firm, consistent, and reasonable control and close supervision, provide the optimal environment for the healthy and competent development of children". This type of parenting seems especially important for children dealing with multiple marital divorces and remarriages. In addition, adolescents who experienced both parental support and monitoring expressed lower levels of externalizing and internalizing behaviors.

Most children live with their custodial mothers. Yet, little evidence suggests that mother-, father- or joint-custody offers greater advantages over the other. Father-custody homes pertain largely to older boys who have mothers with lower levels of education and financial means and who might suffer from psychological problems. Some studies claim that same-sex custody arrangements benefit children during adolescence. Custodial fathers tend to have fewer problems with disciplining their children and can often offer better financial means. Nevertheless, they also tend to have a more reserved relationship with their children and monitor their children's activities less carefully. Girls in mother-custody homes often develop close relationships with their mothers and serve as a source of support. In general, children living in single-custody households grow up more quickly, because they receive greater autonomy in decision-making and responsibility. Oftentimes, they help with household tasks, take care of siblings, and help their parents with problems.

Boys tend to accept stepfathers more readily than girls and benefit more from having a new father figure in the household than do girls.

Noncustodial fathers and mothers differ significantly in their involvement with their children. Noncustodial mothers usually try to keep contact and tend to play a larger role of emotional support in their children's lives. They oftentimes live nearby and sustain close relationships that address their children's needs. In contrast, noncustodial fathers uphold contact and pay child support only if they "feel they have control over decisions about their children and when conflict is low". Only about 25 percent of fathers visit their children on a weekly basis and 20 percent of fathers have no contact or see their children just a few times a year. They usually have a more distant relationship with their children and mostly engage in recreational activities but do not address their children's emotional needs. As a result, "children generally report feeling closer to noncustodial mothers than noncustodial fathers". Overall, children benefit from regular contact with their noncustodial parents. Boys especially do better in school and exhibit less externalizing and internalizing problems when they have contact with their noncustodial fathers.

Co-parenting provides the most advantages for children as parents make important decisions regarding their children together based on mutual understanding and trust. However, few families can achieve these optimal conditions. Many parents engage in parallel parenting without communicating with the other parent. Others do not cooperate at all. As a result, studies do not suggest significant advantages of joint-custody arrangements.

Supportive and authoritative relationships between stepchildren and stepparents benefit the adjustment of children. However, many children do not feel comfortable opening up to their stepparents. In addition, the lack of biological relatedness can also undermine the formation of close relationships. Boys tend to accept stepfathers more readily than girls and benefit more from having a new father figure in the household than do girls.

Children should know the causes for their parents' divorce and have a say in their living arrangements and have the freedom to decide how much contact they would like to have with their noncustodial parents.

Extra-familial Factors

Children from divorced families have a higher chance of experiencing peer pressure and becoming part of destructive peer groups, because they tend to have lower self-esteem and social competence than children from non-divorced families. Many adolescents distance themselves from their families and seek other activities outside the home. This often leads them to engage in delinquent behavior and increases the risk of early pregnancy and substance abuse. In contrast, other adolescents receive support from close friends or from youth groups and organizations. Furthermore, studies show that children who have caring, non-parental adults who serve as role models such as mentors, coaches, and neighbors in their lives can cope better when they experience a lack of parental support at home.

Children with positive attachments to their schools often cope better with their new life circumstances. School environments characterized by "defined schedules, rules, and regulations, and the use of warm, consistent discipline and expectations for mature behavior have been associated with enhanced social and cognitive development in children from divorced and remarried families". Children with behavioral problems and unstable family situations receive the greatest benefits from supportive schools and teachers.

Legal mediations have increased joint-custody arrangements, which have led to greater financial support and involvement from noncustodial fathers. However, the positive results of these interventions do not seem significant to the well-being of children. Nevertheless, many children appreciate the continued role of their fathers in their lives.

Interventions should primarily promote effective family processes such as parental support and monitoring. Educational programs for parents can largely contribute to these goals by giving parents the tools to cope with the stresses associated with divorce to limit conflict and to practice successful parenting. Furthermore, youth groups and other pro-social organizations such as church groups can serve as a strong source of support for children and adolescents. Authoritative schooling can particularly help children with externalizing behavioral problems by setting regulations and rules. Strengthening intra-family and extended family support can contribute to family resilience and buffer children's risk factors following divorce. Lastly, children should know the causes for their parents' divorce and have a say in their living arrangements and have the freedom to decide how much contact they would like to have with their noncustodial parents.

Divorce exposes children to many risk factors such as high conflict, the loss of important relationships, and remarriage. This can lead these children to develop externalizing and internalizing behaviors. For many years, some couples did not dare to divorce because they feared the detrimental effects on their children, although divorce would have been the most beneficial solution for everyone involved. Media and certain studies strengthened this view. Now, however, most researchers would agree that most children have the necessary resilience to deal with their new circumstances and challenges and ultimately become well-adjusted adults. Internal protective factors such as temperament and coping skills as well as good parenting and a supportive environment help these children successfully cope with their new situation. Future directions for research on divorce should examine the varying degrees of resilience of children from different cultural, ethnic, and socioeconomic heritages. This could help in creating intervention programs tailored to the specific needs of families with different backgrounds. Studies should use standardized measures and employ representative samples to make them reliable and valid. In addition, interventions should focus primarily on improving good parenting practices as they represent the most important factor in the adjustment of children.

2

Divorce Affects Young Children Differently than Adolescents

Carl Pickhardt

Carl Pickhardt is a psychologist in Austin, Texas. He is the author of Surviving Your Child's Adolescence, The Connected Father, *and* The Future of Your Only Child.

No matter the child's age, divorce introduces a massive change in his or her life. However, responses can be different if the child is young or an adolescent. Children are dependent, and divorce can undermine their dependency on their parents, while dividing the family creates unfamiliarity, insecurity, and instability. To feel more connected, they may display regressive behaviors in order to elicit parental concern and bring their parents back together. On the other hand, adolescents are independent—in a divorce, they may display aggressive behaviors and resolve to rely more on themselves. To get back at their parents and cope with the loss of trust, adolescents may disregard discipline and become increasingly self-interested.

In response to my blog about single parenting adolescents, I received this email request: "I was wondering if you could address the effects of divorce on very small children."

What I can do is try to distinguish some general ways children (up through about age 8 or 9) often react to parental divorce in contrast to how adolescents (beginning around ages 9–13) often respond. Understand that I am talking here about tendencies, not certainties.

Divorce introduces a massive change into the life of a boy or girl no matter what the age. Witnessing loss of love between parents, having parents break their marriage commitment, adjusting to going back and forth between two different households, and the daily absence of one parent while living with the other, all create a challenging new family circumstance in which to live. In the personal history of the boy or girl, parental divorce is a watershed event. Life that follows is significantly changed from how life was before.

[The child] relies on wishful thinking to help allay the pain of loss, holding onto hope for a parental reunion much longer than does the adolescent who is quicker to accept the finality of this unwelcome family change.

Somewhat different responses to this painful turn of events occur if the boy or girl is still in childhood or has entered adolescence. Basically, divorce tends to intensify the child's dependence and it tends to accelerate the adolescent's independence; it often elicits a more regressive response in the child and a more aggressive response in the adolescent. Consider why this variation may be so.

The child's world is a dependent one, closely connected to parents who are favored companions, heavily reliant on parental care, with family the major locus of one's social life. The adolescent world is a more independent one, more separated and distant from parents, more self-sufficient, where friends have become favored companions, and where the major locus of one's social life now extends outside of family into a larger world of life experience.

For the young child, divorce shakes trust in dependency on parents who now behave in an extremely undependable way. They surgically divide the family unit into two different households between which the child must learn to transit back and forth, for a while creating unfamiliarity, instability, and insecurity, never being able to be with one parent without having to be apart from the other.

Convincing a young child of the permanence of divorce can be hard when his intense longing fantasizes that somehow, some way, mom and dad will be living back together again someday. He relies on wishful thinking to help allay the pain of loss, holding onto hope for a parental reunion much longer than does the adolescent who is quicker to accept the finality of this unwelcome family change. Thus parents who put in a joint presence at special family celebrations and holiday events to recreate family closeness for the child only feed the child's fantasy and delay his adjustment.

The Dependent Child's Reaction

The dependent child's short term reaction to divorce can be an anxious one. So much is different, new, unpredictable, and unknown that life becomes filled with scary questions? "What is going to happen next?" "Who will take care of me?" "If my parents can lose [love] for each other, can they lose love for me?" "With one parent moving out, what if I lose the other too?" Answering such worry questions with worst fears, the child's response can be regressive.

The more independent-minded adolescent tends to deal more aggressively to divorce, often reacting in a mad, rebellious way, more resolved to disregard family discipline and take care of himself.

By reverting to a former way of functioning, more parental care-taking may be forthcoming. There can be separation anxieties, crying at bed times, breaking toilet training, bedwetting, clinging, whining, tantrums, and temporary loss of established self-care skills, all of which can compel parental attention.

The child wants to feel more connected in a family situation where a major disconnection has occurred. Regression to earlier dependency can partly be an effort to elicit parental concern, bringing them close when divorce has pulled each of them further away—the resident parent now busier and more preoccupied, the absent parent simply less available because of being less around.

The Independent Adolescent's Reaction

The more independent-minded adolescent tends to deal more aggressively to divorce, often reacting in a mad, rebellious way, more resolved to disregard family discipline and take care of himself since parents have failed to keep commitments to family that were originally made.

Where the child may have tried to get parents back, the adolescent may try to get back at parents. Where the child felt grief, the adolescence has a grievance. "If they can't be trusted to stay together and take care of the family, then I need to start relying more on myself." "If they can break their marriage and put themselves first, then I can put myself first too." "If they don't mind hurting me, then I don't mind hurting them."

Now the adolescent can act aggressively to take control of his life by behaving even more distantly and defiantly, more determined to live his life his way, more dedicated to his self-interest than before. He feels increasingly autonomous in a family situation that feels disconnected. He now feels more impelled and entitled to act on his own.

For the parent who divorces with an adolescent, the young person's increased dedication to self-interest must be harnessed by insisting on increased responsibility as more separation and independence from family occurs.

For the parent who divorces with a child, the priority is establishing a sense of family order and predictability. This means observing the three R's required to restore a child's trust in security, familiarity, and dependency—Routines, Rituals, and Reassurance.

Thus parents establish household and visitation Routines so the child knows what to expect. They allow the child to create Rituals to feel more in control of her life. And they provide continual Reassurance that the parents are as lovingly connected to the child as ever, and are committed to making this new family arrangement work.

3

Cohabitation Has Replaced Divorce as Biggest Threat to Children

Dave Bohon

Dave Bohon is a writer for The New American, *a conservative biweekly magazine.*

Cohabitation, in which unmarried couples have children and live together, is a bigger threat to children than divorce. Increasing fourteen-fold since 1970, the percentage of children that lived in cohabiting households by age twelve is now 42 percent, compared to 24 percent that lived in divorced households. The heightened instability of cohabitation increases children's risk of experiencing physical, emotional, financial, and social problems; they have higher rates of externalizing and internalizing disorders, aggression, and depression than children in married households. Disproportionately affecting the poor, the trend is also migrating into lower-middle-class families, further weakening vulnerable and marginalized communities.

A new report from a pair of organizations dedicated to strengthening the institution of marriage shows that an alarming number of U.S. couples are deciding to have children without being married—a decision that places those children at risk for physical, emotional, financial, and other social problems.

The study, released by the National Marriage Project and the Institute for American Values, found that while, toward the end of the 20th century, "divorce posed the biggest threat to marriage in the United States," in today's world "the rise of cohabiting households with children is the largest unrecognized threat to the quality and stability of children's family lives."

The report noted that "because of the growing prevalence of cohabitation, which has risen fourteen-fold since 1970, today's children are much more likely to spend time in a cohabiting household than they are to see their parents divorce." In fact, according to the National Survey of Family Growth, compiled by the federal Centers for Disease Control, by the age of 12 a staggering 42 percent of children have lived with co-habiting parents, a number that dwarfs the 24 percent of children who have lived with divorced parents.

Research shows that cohabitating couples are twice as likely to split as married couples.

Statistics show that "more children are currently born to cohabiting couples than to single mothers," the report noted. "Another 20 percent or so of children spend time in a cohabiting household with an unrelated adult at some point later in their childhood, often after their parents marriage breaks down. This means that more than four in ten children are exposed to a cohabiting relationship."

Dr. W. Bradford Wilcox of the National Marriage Project and the study's lead author observed that "the divorce rate for married couples with children has returned almost to the levels we saw before the divorce revolution kicked in during the 1970s. Nevertheless, family instability is on the rise for American children as a whole. This seems in part to be because more couples are having children in cohabiting unions, which are very unstable."

Wilcox told National Public Radio that the marital conflict depicted in the classic 1979 film *Kramer vs. Kramer* is no longer representative of relationship dysfunction in America. It's now *"Kramer vs. Kramer vs. Johnson and Nelson,"* he quipped. "We're moving into a pattern where we're seeing more instability, more adults moving in and out of the household in this relationship carousel."

According to Wilcox, Americans who grew up during the 1970s and '80s divorce epidemic were conditioned to hold marriage at arms' length, postponing it even after having children. But research shows that cohabiting couples are twice as likely to split as married couples. "Ironically," he told NPR, "they're likely to experience even more instability than they would [have] if they had taken the time and effort to move forward slowly and get married before starting a family."

A surge in couples cohabitating and having children began to dominate poor communities in the late 1960s, but the trend has now migrated into lower middle-class families in America.

NPR cited another study showing that a quarter of American women with more than one child had those children with multiple partners. Psychologist John Gottman, co-author of the National Marriage Project report, said that such instability has a major negative impact on kids of those relationships. "Both in externalizing disorders, more aggression, and internalizing disorders, more depression," he said, "children of cohabiting couples are at greater risk than children of married couples."

The study, which surveyed more than 250 peer-reviewed journal articles on marriage and family life in the U.S. and elsewhere, noted that children of cohabiting parents are more likely than those from traditional married families to face such emotional and social problems as drug abuse, depression, dropping out of high school, physical and sexual abuse, and poverty.

As reported by the Catholic News Agency, the study also found that "family stability is part of a class divide. Children from college-educated homes have seen their family lives stabilize, while children from less-educated homes have seen their lives become increasingly unstable."

Observed Wilcox: "There's a two-family model emerging in American life. The educated and affluent enjoy relatively strong, stable families. Everyone else is more likely to be consigned to unstable, unworkable ones."

The report noted that a surge in couples cohabitating and having children began to dominate poor communities in the late 1960s, but the trend has now migrated into lower middle-class families in America. "Out-of-wedlock births among white women with a high school diploma rose more than sixfold in recent decades," the *New York Times* cited the report, "jumping to 34 percent in the late 2000s, from 5 percent in 1982. In contrast, the rate for white college graduates stayed flat at about 2 percent."

"While births to white women in cohabiting relationships rose by about two-thirds from the early 1990s to the mid-2000s, the proportion jumped by about half for black women and nearly doubled for Hispanic women, though that increase was affected by a large influx of immigrants," continued the *Times,* quoting Sheela Kennedy, a research associate at the Minnesota Population Center. "There's growing evidence that families that would be unstable anyway are just skipping marriage," said Kennedy, suggesting that cohabitation may be as much a symptom of instability in the lives of children as it is a cause.

Nonetheless, the study's authors insisted, an intact marriage between a child's biological parents remains the "gold standard" for successful families. "Children are most likely to thrive economically, socially, and psychologically, in this family form," declared the Institute for American Values in a statement about the study.

The study's authors contended that the benefits of marriage are not reserved for just the wealthy and educated, but "extend to poor, working-class, and minority communities, despite the fact that marriage has weakened in these communities in the last four decades."

The study concluded that whether society succeeds or fails "in building a healthy marriage culture is clearly a matter of legitimate public concern and an issue of paramount importance if we wish to reverse the marginalization of the most vulnerable members of our society: the working class, the poor, minorities, and children."

4

Divorce Has Unique Impacts on Special Needs Children

Barbara Epperson

Based in Houston, Texas, Barbara Epperson is an attorney with experience in family law and the field of special education.

Children with disabilities have unique needs that divorcing parents and their lawyers must address and collaborate to meet. The four critical issues are visitation agreements and transitions between homes; decisions regarding education; health and medical care; and opportunities for socializing and recreation. In arranging visitation, parents should minimize disruption and focus on longer, more concentrated visits. Placement in appropriate educational programs and schools is also the task of both parents. For their children's specialized medical care and therapies, parents must agree on involvement in decision-making and sharing information. And finding social opportunities also poses a challenge, requiring parental cooperation to identify sufficient activities.

Each year, parents of a million American children divorce. Divorce affects everyone involved, but it is often the most difficult for children with disabilities. When custody determinations or modifications involve children with disabilities, the decisions regarding the "best interests of the child" can be even more complex.

Barbara Epperson, "When Parents of Children with Disabilities Divorce," *GPSOLO*, May/June 2010. Copyright © 2010 American Journal of Law. All rights reserved. Reproduced with permission.

The words "best interests of the child" have no one, single meaning, and the laws in most states define "best interests" by listing a number of factors for the court to consider. Common factors in many states include the following: the capacity of the parents to understand and meet the needs of the child; religion and/or cultural considerations; the child's wishes; the need for continuation of a stable home environment; the relationship between the child and parents, siblings, and others important in his or her life; the child's adjustment to school and community; the age and sex of the child; and parental use of excessive discipline or emotional abuse.

> *For a child with a disability, it is sometimes better to minimize frequent adjustments to a new environment . . . and focus on structuring longer visits with each parent for more concentrated time.*

Unique Needs of Children with Disabilities

Because all children are unique and respond differently to divorce, lawyers should become familiar with the characteristics of all children in the family—including any child with a disability—such as the children's age, emotional maturity, resiliency to change, and ability to cope with changes in family structure during and after the finalization of the divorce. Divorcing parents need to recognize more than just their legal responsibility and be willing to adjust the environment to make it ideal for the child to grow and mature.

Lawyers assisting clients who have children with disabilities should focus on resolving the following critical issues: (1) visitation agreements and transitions between homes; (2) educational decision making; (3) health and medical care, including special therapies; and (4) social and recreational opportunities.

In some families, parents do not agree about how to address the unique needs of a child with a disability. Sometimes, one parent may be in denial about the existence of a disability or may not agree with the other parent regarding the best approach needed to care for or seek appropriate supports and services to meet the needs of that child. In those cases, lawyers should consider engaging neutral professionals who can guide the decision-making process and offer alternative solutions to "typical" visitation arrangements. Professionals may also make suggestions about how to obtain consensus regarding any care or treatment the child may need.

Visitation and Child Care Arrangements

Typical visitation arrangements for children of divorcing parents (whether the children have a disability or not) involve alternating weekends and/or midweek visits, as well as extended school holiday and summer visits. For a child with a disability, it is sometimes better to minimize frequent adjustments to a new environment, especially during the school year, and focus on structuring longer visits with each parent for more concentrated time. For many children with disabilities, especially children diagnosed with autism, a disruption to their daily routine can affect behavior and school performance and result in unnecessary stress for both the children and parents. Parents should communicate to minimize disruptions or changes in routines. This will ensure that the routines in each household complement each other and serve to avoid any negative impact on the child.

> *The task of finding appropriate educational supports and social outlets is often a challenge for parents of children with disabilities.*

Divorcing parents should take a similarly thoughtful approach to child care arrangements. The parent with whom the child lives may need to seek out temporary respite care to give that parent a break; finding a trusted babysitter or child care facility that is able to respond to the unique needs of a child with a disability is often challenging. With respect to these arrangements, divorcing parents should strive to minimize last-minute changes. Even slight alterations, such a those associated with a different pickup location, a different pickup time, or a new babysitter, may result in unnecessary disruption to routines and create anxiety for the child involved. Even as the child grows into adulthood, this may continue to be an issue. Children with disabilities often need supervised care even as they get older. For example, a child with developmental disabilities who cannot function without supervision will need assistance in most aspects of daily living activities such as bathing, dressing, feeding, and/or social interactions with others.

Educational Considerations

Children with disabilities should be afforded the same opportunities as children without disabilities when it involves educational programming, social opportunities, and the ability to be as independent as possible. Families often struggle to overcome barriers that serve to exclude a child with a disability in school and social settings. To promote inclusion, parents must work together to seek opportunities for the child to participate in school and social events.

The task of finding appropriate educational supports and social outlets is often a challenge for parents of children with disabilities. Divorcing parents should collaborate in selecting appropriate educational programs and making decisions, taking into consideration the time needed to research the appropriateness of the program, the supports that the school is suggesting, and other supports outside of the school day, such as tutoring or structured remediation that will support learning.

If the child is of school age and qualifies for special education, the school system will identify the disability under the eligibility criteria outlined in the Individuals with Disabilities

Education Improvement Act of 2004, Public Law 108-446, 20 USC §1400. This law provides individualized services to students in public schools and emphasizes inclusion of students with disabilities to the extent possible with non-disabled peers. Children who are identified with a disability, and who need services, receive an Individualized Education Program (IEP), which includes making decisions on academic goals, placement, accommodations, assessments, and other needed supports. The IEP is developed with input from both school personnel and the family and is based on the child's present levels of performance.

For other students whose disabilities may require more minor support related to their education, Section 504 of the Rehabilitation Act of 1973 provides eligible students with accommodations and modifications to assist them in the school environment. Section 504 is a civil rights law that prohibits discrimination against individuals with disabilities and ensures that the child with a disability has equal access to an education. Under this law parents also participate in meetings where appropriate placement and services are determined.

Medical treatments and therapies are often part of the daily routine for parents who have a child with a disability.

The family law attorney should obtain school records that document the disability and describe the educational program that has been designed to meet the unique needs of the child. These school records can often be used to illustrate why any request that deviates from prescribed child support guidelines or a standard possession order is appropriate. At a minimum, records should be reviewed for the following: 1) the individual assessment report that includes test scores for both intellectual functioning levels as well as academic performance levels; 2) behavioral information and suggestions for instructional approaches that address the unique needs of the child; 3) any medical records that document the disability and outline prescribed treatment; 4) the current IEP; and 5) additional reports such as psychological reports, speech evaluations, assistive technology evaluations, functional behavioral evaluations, occupational therapy evaluations, and physical therapy evaluations.

These records provide substantial information related to the nature of the disability and offer a prognosis for improvement and recommendations for needed supports. This information is valuable in helping parents to develop a child-centered visitation plan that focuses on the best interests of the child.

It is important for divorcing parents to have a final divorce decree that clearly states which parent will make educational decisions, or in cases where these decisions are shared, how parents can overcome an impasse when disagreements occur. Precise drafting helps guide the decision-making process so as not to delay needed services.

Medical Decisions

Medical treatments and therapies are often part of the daily routine for parents who have a child with a disability. For children with medical conditions such as cerebral palsy, orthopedic impairments, or serious health conditions, critical decisions include obtaining ongoing medical care, administering medication, making periodic appointments with health care professionals to monitor physical conditions, and granting consent to invasive procedures. Because needed medical services may be more frequent and involve additional expense, parents need to agree about who makes decisions involving invasive procedures, how each parent is included in the decision-making process, and how information is shared when needed medical services are recommended by the child's physician. In many cases, other services such as counseling, physical or occupational therapy, speech therapy, or other specialized treatments are needed for children with disabilities. Emphasis on careful drafting regarding medical decisions is very important.

Many students with learning disabilities, emotional disabilities, or physical disabilities are successful in continuing their education after high school graduation.

Social and Recreational Opportunities

Parents should work together to locate appropriate social and recreational activities for children with disabilities. In addition to familiar activities such as scouting, organized sports, or other children's events, many communities offer specialized, structured activities for children with disabilities such as art classes, swimming, or camps that match these children's unique needs.

When researching social opportunities, parents should consider whether the adults involved have experience working with children who have disabilities and whether these social or recreational programs will include the child with children who do not have disabilities. Parents should also work together to maintain the schedule for social and recreational activities and be flexible with visitation so that the child participates on a regular basis. Transportation to and from activities may require more coordination between parents for the benefit of the child.

Adulthood and Continuing Support

As children mature, parents should also work together to explore options for post-secondary education and training, employment, independent living, and other goals for the future. Planning for the future will require an organized approach to locating community supports, completing applications, developing interviewing skills, and practicing self-advocacy skills. Many students with learning disabilities, emotional disabilities, or physical disabilities are successful in continuing their education after high school graduation, owing in part to supports at post-secondary institutions and high expectations for their ability to become self-sufficient.

Children with disabilities need the continued support of both parents after a divorce. Custody and visitation plans that focus on the best interest of the child must consider school programs, transitions between households, the opportunity for the child to participate in community and leisure activities, and flexibility for visitation that lets the children keep appointments for special therapy, counseling sessions, or other medical care. In preparing for life after high school, parents should work together to identify a career path and adult living arrangements that will support the child as he or she continues to grow and mature into adulthood. For children with severe disabilities, who require continuous care and supervision owing to developmental or physical delays, parental support will continue into adulthood. Those parents will also need information about estate planning, available health insurance, and Social Security benefits that can help provide a secure future for their child.

5

Parents Must Manage Their Children's Anger over Divorce

Thalia Ferenc

Thalia Ferenc is a clinical social worker and therapist based in Charlevoix, Michigan.

During divorce, anger is common among most children, who may feel powerless, afraid, or furious at parents for being the source of pain rather than protection from it. However, few openly direct their anger at parents but instead channel it into unacceptable behavior or emotional problems. Parents should encourage children to express their feelings in words—or without words if children are unable to attach any to their feelings. Furthermore, they should not let anger over divorce excuse children for acting out of bounds. To avoid the blame trap, parents should also recognize that children may behave badly around the parent to whom they are most attached.

Anger is a common emotion felt by most children during their parents' divorce transition. Kids seldom want their family and their familiar home to disintegrate beneath them. They often feel powerless, afraid and furious that parents who are supposed to protect them from pain, seem to be the source of it. Some children express their anger as rage, while others withdraw or become depressed. Often the anger is never openly directed at the parents themselves, at least not about the separation or divorce. Instead, there are more frequent

Thalia Ferenc, "Managing Children's Anger About Divorce or Separation," Education .com, May 7, 2014. Copyright © 2014 National Association of Social Workers. All rights reserved. Reproduced with permission.

and intense fights between siblings or playmates. There may be more oppositional behavior around ordinary and reasonable expectations by authority figures at home, school or both. Frequently heard is the classic parent-wounding epithet: "I hate you!" Or the child may spend all his or her time hiding in the bedroom with music or TV, phone, computer or electronic games.

What's a Parent to Do?

Many parents fail to recognize the underlying source of the outrageous behavior and clamp down with groundings and assorted punishments "to get the kid to shape up." Parents are even sometimes inclined to take the anger personally and feel unloved and unappreciated. Neither of these choices will help the child through this difficult time. Children (and adults) need to learn to express their feelings, including anger, in a constructive way. Using words will do nicely. Reflect back what is seen and heard through sentences such as, "You seem to be pretty angry at me lately." Or "You sound furious right now." It is always best to keep one's voice even and in an understanding tone, rather [than] accusatory. Listen for as long as s/he is willing to talk. Children need to know that someone cares enough to hear them out.

It is commonplace for the child to act up for the parent with whom he feels most secure.

Encourage Feeling Expression in Words

Empathize by letting her know most kids would feel as she does, and, in fact, if you were the kid in this situation, you might feel the same way, too. You may hear only about the unfairness of your TV watching rules, but discharging this anger by talking about it calmly will prepare the way for other discussions about the separation, and will lighten her anger load to make the rest just a little more bearable. Helping children identify the feelings, and then come up with their own workable solutions to the problems, gives them a sense of power. A sense of power and control is often lost when children are in the midst of a divorce. Children can become proactive and find solutions they can implement themselves. Allowing solutions to be voiced, brings a sense of control back to the children.

Encourage Feeling Expression Without Words

Children often do not know the words to attach to the feelings they are experiencing. Use words that help them identify feelings are: sad, frustrated, upset, scared, mad. Sometimes, using drawings or illustrations of facial expressions of feelings will help. Make sure they have lots of opportunities for physical activity. This can release tension and help them better able to handle stressful situations. Art activities that do not require a specific product are very effective ways to express emotion. This means that coloring books or a craft project that is supposed to look a certain way, while they may be fun, will not produce expression. Using clay or glue with small, odd pieces of wood, paint and drawing with markers on blank paper will do a better job. Finger painting, with special paints or with pudding on a cookie sheet is fun and releases feelings as well. While parents may be tempted to ask the child what the object they have created is, it is better to discuss the feelings that went into the project or what the project may represent. Many children will simply make something up in order to have an answer for you. You might comment, "Tell me about your drawing. It looks like you worked hard on it." Some of these methods can be used to handle angry, unacceptable behavior.

Limit Out of Bounds Angry Behavior

None of this is meant to excuse behavior that is out of bounds. Swearing, biting, hitting, breaking things, screaming are not acceptable. Parents can say, "I understand you're angry, but this is not behavior I will tolerate. I want to talk to you about how you're feeling, but you need to go to your room to cool off until you can talk more calmly." Then make sure to seek him out to ask if he wants to talk about the problem afterwards. Even if he doesn't, the door is open for future discussions and validated that his feelings are important.

Avoid the Blame Trap

It is commonplace for the child to act up for the parent with whom he feels most secure. Usually, this translates into good behavior with the parent who is gone, since he may not be sure it is safe to show negative feelings to someone who could leave him so easily. The sense of blame that may result only serves to distract the parent from the real problem of helping the child cope with change. In talking with the other parent about the child's anger problems, develop a plan that both will follow to help the child express and manage the feelings in appropriate ways.

6

When Parents Divorce They Must Emotionally Support Their Children

William Mosier

William Mosier is a marriage and family therapist, professor of child development at Wright State University, and director of research at the Lynda A. Cohen Center for the Study of Child Development in Dayton, Ohio.

Children require the emotional support of both parents during and after a divorce, as it can have lasting impacts. While parents cannot make the realities of the situation painless, they can follow several guidelines to make it less traumatic. For instance, parents should resist talking with children about the divorce when emotions are volatile and reassure them that they are not responsible for it. Moreover, parents should not use children as pawns in power struggles and put pressure on them to adapt quickly to painful changes. Because it can erode children's self-confidence, parents should also help them feel loved and wanted through maintaining an open relationship and encouraging them to express their worries and concerns.

During and after divorce, children need the emotional support of both parents. When parents are going through a divorce, the stressfulness of the situation can be complicated. Both parents love their children and don't want them to suffer

William Mosier, "During and After Divorce: Children Need the Emotional Support of Both Parents," *Annals of Psychotherapy and Integrative Health*, vol. 16, no. 3, Fall 2013, p. 82. Copyright © 2013 American Psychotherapy Association. All rights reserved. Reproduced with permission.

from the parent's decision to seek a divorce. However, in spite of parent commitment to protecting their children from emotional trauma that could result from parental divorce, far too often divorce can leave a lasting scar on children. This raises several questions:

- How should the situation be handled to minimize the negative impact of divorce on children?

- What can parents do to help their children cope with, what seems like, the death of their family?

- How should parents tell the children about their decision to divorce?

A divorce or marital separation does not end one's responsibilities as a parent. Children need the affection and attention of both parents. As emotionally stressful as the situation is for the adults involved, the situation is even more stressful for the children. The way a parent expresses his or her feelings about the situation, as well as the way the parent behaves around the children while attempting to cope with the ordeal, will affect the way the children will feel, not only about the divorce, but also about themselves. The impact of the experience will tend to affect the children even into adulthood.

Parents must reassure children they are not responsible for the divorce.

Talking About the Divorce

Once parents have made the decision to divorce, there is nothing that will make the reality of divorce painless for the kids; however, there are guidelines that can help a parent handle this difficult situation in a manner that can be less traumatic for the children. Consider the following:

- Parents should resist the impulse to talk with their children about the divorce at times when emotions are volatile. Parents especially should avoid telling them about the decision to seek a divorce when feeling angry. It is a topic of discussion that requires calm actions on the part of the parent. Any discussion of the divorce must be done in a way that reassures the children their parents' love for them will continue.

- If at all possible children should receive the news from both parents together, not from each parent separately. This approach helps to reduce blame and to reassure the children that both parents love them. It can help the children to understand their parents are not getting a divorce from them but from each other.

- Parents should keep the details of what led to their "break-up" fairly general. Kids will be curious, but parents do not owe children a detailed explanation as to why they have decided to divorce. Parents need to keep the ages of their children in mind when attempting to tell them what happened and why the decision was made. Too much detail only will cause more confusion for younger children.

- Parents must reassure children they are not responsible for the divorce. Young children tend to blame themselves for everything that happens around them. They need kind words and caring gestures that will help them to feel safe, that they are still loved, and that the divorce was not their fault.

- Each parent must accept responsibility for the decision to separate and divorce; don't pass the buck as this will tend to make the children more fearful the divorce is their fault.

- If the decision is final, parents need to be honest. Parents should not indicate the decision might be reversible. Children should not be offered a false hope of reconciliation unless that is truly a possibility.

- Parents need to let the children know how the divorce will impact their lives, including when they will see the parent who will no longer be living in the home.

- Parents must be very careful to refrain from voicing criticism about the children's other parent. Expressing bitterness only will leave children with deep scars that cannot be easily erased, as the children grow older. Parents need to avoid involving the children in any unresolved problems they are having with the other parent. Children should never be used as pawns in the power struggles between their parents. Children should not be forced to take sides in the game: "Who is right, and who is wrong." This is not the children's divorce. It is a problem between the parents and should stay with the parents.

- Parents should not put pressure on children to adjust quickly to the situation. Children need to be allowed time for adjustment to such a significantly painful change in their world.

- Parents should avoid too many disruptions to their children's daily routines. Children need a sense of security that comes with established routines.

- Parents must reinforce the attitude of unconditional love for their children. The adults in their lives need to make sure the children understand they are not being rejected or abandoned by their parents.

- Parents must guard against their guilt leading to over-permissiveness. Children need persistently consistent guidance. They need and want to have clearly set limits. They need to know what is expected of them. Children feel more secure when clear limits are set and maintained, especially during times of uncomfortable change.

Children Need Love and Acceptance

Divorce usually means everyone loses. This is true for the children even more so than for the adults. The behavior a child observes in his or her parents has the strongest influence on the child's emotional adjustment to divorce.

Divorce can cause a child's self-confidence to erode. Therefore, it is important for both parents to help restore their children's self-confidence by helping the children feel wanted and loved. When parents maintain an open relationship with their children and the children feel loved and accepted, they will be able to more easily overcome the shock of marital separation and divorce and be able to re-focus on the uniqueness of the relationship they have with each parent.

Avoiding thinking of divorce as the death of a family is vital to helping children remain resilient after a divorce. Although divorce leaves a lasting impact on a family, it does not destroy it. Rather, divorce forces a restructuring of the family that, for better or worse, will change the dynamics of the family. The change will be irreversible; however, the role of a parent continues after divorce; fulfilling the parenting responsibilities just becomes more complicated.

Under the pressure of divorce, family relationships can become strained. Divorce is a major trauma in the life of a child. Parents can help their children through this trying time by encouraging them to openly express their worries and concerns. This will help to reassure the children their parents' love is absolute and unconditional.

7

Divorced Parents Must Work to Coparent Their Children

Matthew Sullivan

Based in Palo Alto, California, Matthew Sullivan practices forensic psychology and is on the board of directors of the Association of Family and Conciliation Courts.

Coparenting is when divorced adults share the responsibilities of raising children in shared-custody arrangements; its essential functions are to exchange child-focused information and engage in child-focused decision-making. There are three models of coparenting. Cooperative parents have accurate perceptions of themselves and each other and show trust and good problem-solving skills. Chronically conflicted coparents have misperceptions of themselves and each other and show mistrust and poor problem-solving skills. Parallel coparenting is characterized by low engagement between parents and can reduce conflict and benefit children if child-focused information exchanges and decision-making are sufficient. As the most common model, parallel coparenting serves the interest of children in most situations, particularly when communication is conducted online and in a businesslike manner.

In addition to the other role relationships that may exist between parents—romantic partners, business partners, friends, etc.—when individuals have a child together, they become coparents for life. Coparenting is "a shared activity undertaken by adults responsible for the care and upbringing of children."

Raising children in a shared-custody situation, which implies shared decision-making and shared parenting time, is an enduring partnership that is critical to a child's development. After divorce, the nuclear family becomes a binuclear family—two households instead of one. The healthy "raising" of children requires an adequate environment in the two respective homes (good enough parenting) and adequate functioning between homes (good enough coparenting).

The two essential functions of coparenting are (1) a child-focused information exchange between parents and (2) child-focused decision-making. Transitions in the structure of the coparenting relationship, such as those that occur with the birth of siblings, work-related changes, children becoming school age, and the launching of children into their later adolescence, can challenge and impair functional coparenting.

The most robust finding in the divorce literature over the last 30 years is that high-conflict shared custody arrangements damage children's healthy development.

Regardless of the challenges that may impact the parents during these life transitions, the continuation of functional coparenting is essential. After separation and divorce, coparents can and should choose a structure of coparenting that meets the demands and needs of their shared-custody situation. They cannot, however, opt out of this coparenting partnership without compromising the long-term adjustment of their children.

Toxic Agents: Interparental Conflict and Court Involvement

Many coparents fail to establish a workable shared-custody situation for their children as they move from a nuclear family to binuclear family system. Their inability to move on from the anger and blame that accompanies the loss of their spousal relationship often obstructs their ability to create a workable shared-custody structure (a parenting plan) without involvement in the adversarial legal process.

Litigants don't make good coparents, and parents' exposure to adversarial court processes often exacerbates conflict and renders them incapable of implementing their parenting plans. These high-conflict coparents continue to use any engagement to keep the fires of contempt and blame burning, to the detriment of their children.

The most robust finding in the divorce literature over the last 30 years is that high-conflict shared custody arrangements damage children's healthy development. Unfortunately, absent a decision to abandon their parental roles, coparents are forced to find a way, preferably without the toxic effects of conflict and/or continued court involvement, to functionally coparent.

Models of Coparenting: Choose Wisely

There are three basic models of coparenting in shared-custody situations: cooperative, conflicted, and parallel. In cooperative coparenting relationships, the exchange of child-focused information and child-focused decision-making are easier to accomplish.

1. Cooperative coparents, characterized in studies as roughly 25% of coparents, are described as (a) having accurate perceptions of themselves, of their coparent, and of their child; (b) trusting their coparent; and (c) having good problem-solving skills to negotiate differences as they make child-focused decisions. Long-term outcomes for their children are good.

2. Chronically conflicted coparents are characterized by (a) significant distortions in their perceptions of self, in their coparent, and in their child; (b) mistrust of their coparent; and (c) insufficient problem-solving and decision-making skills. Chronically conflicted coparents

have children who are significantly more likely to have long-term adjustment problems than children who are raised in shared-custody situations with cooperative co-parents.

3. Parallel coparenting is the most common model in shared-custody situations. It is characterized by a low level of engagement between parents. In shared-custody situations, low engagement can reduce the conflict between parents and thus benefit children, as long as it fosters adequate information sharing and decision-making about the children.

Interestingly, children raised with coparents who engage in parallel parenting have long-term outcomes similar to children raised by cooperative coparents. This is important because roughly forty percent of coparents in shared-custody situations engage in parallel coparenting.

[A functional communication channel] is essential to coordinating the health, education, and social life of the child as he or she moves between homes.

Successful Parallel Parenting

The essential ingredients of successful coparenting are (1) an appropriate parenting plan or custody order, (2) a functional communication channel between coparents, and (3) a functional decision-making process. In a parallel coparenting model, these should be structured to reduce the amount of engagement (and thus conflict) between coparents while accomplishing the business of coparenting.

The first task in establishing a functional shared-custody arrangement is to create a developmentally appropriate and highly detailed parenting plan. For example, the parenting plan should be so exhaustively detailed in addressing the child's timeshare schedule (regular timeshare, holidays, and summer vacations) that parenting time can be calendared to the minute several months in advance. Similarly, specific protocols that address transitions, phone contact with the noncustodial parent, travel, etc., should be addressed explicitly in the parenting plan. The more detail in the parenting plan, the less engagement between coparents to implement that plan. The less engagement between parents, the less opportunity for conflict; the less conflict, the better for the child.

It is not necessary to reinvent the parenting plan wheel, many resources are available online. See, for example, my website www.california-parentingcooridnator.com and www.afcc.org (the website of the Association of Family and Conciliation Courts) for sample parenting-plan provisions.

The second ingredient of successful coparenting is a functional communication channel between coparents to support the exchange of child-focused information. This information is essential to coordinating the health, education, and social life of the child as he or she moves between homes. Details about homework, illnesses (and their treatment), after-school activities, social engagements, diet, and health are the information that coparents must share.

If implementing a parenting plan through shared decision-making proves impossible, parenting coordination provides an efficient alternative to court involvement.

The BIFF Model

The communication channel between coparents must be structured to support a "business relationship." Bill Eddy, cofounder and president of the High Conflict Institute, LLC, in San Diego, California, provides an excellent set of guidelines for coparenting communication. He recommends the BIFF model—brief, informative, focused, and friendly. Increasingly, such coparents communicate via the Internet—by e-mail and/or a coparenting website. By communicating through cyberspace, they decrease their engagement and any potential for conflict.

Finally, when coparents share legal custody, most decisions related to their children's health, education, extracurricular activities, and social involvement require agreement. This is a tall order for conflicted coparents who are short on problem-solving and negotiation skills and long on reactivity, blame, and disagreement. Getting support through alternative dispute resolution is critical to making the best decisions for your children, containing the conflict with your ex-spouse, and keeping court-involvement in your lives to a minimum.

Parallel Coparenting Plus

Coparenting support is available to assist struggling parents in implementing parallel parenting plans. This support ranges from counseling and mediation, which are typically confidential and advisory, to parenting coordination. Parenting coordination is a non-confidential process in which a delegated court authority steps in to resolve issues in conflict when parents are unable to make joint decisions.

Parenting coordination is a hybrid form of mediation-arbitration, which helps conflicted coparents develop better problem-solving skills and reach agreement about child-related issues. If implementing a parenting plan through shared decision-making proves impossible, parenting coordination provides an efficient alternative to court involvement.

The issues that a parenting coordinator might assist with are not custody and timeshare conflicts, but day-to-day disputes that arise between high-conflict coparents. Parenting coordinators typically address and resolve issues, such as scheduling difficulties (disputes over holiday and vacation schedules), problem transitions, the transfer of clothing, the selection of extracurricular activities, and the introduction of the children to a new significant other.

Parenting coordinators often help structure communication between parents and provide additional support and accountability by monitoring and enforcing rules and promoting businesslike e-mails and the effective use of shared-parenting websites. In addition, parenting coordinators can support the role of mental health and other professionals and nonprofessionals involved with the family. This coordination and support role may interface with the roles of school principals and teachers, tutors, child-care providers, child therapists, physicians and nonprofessionals and community members, such as coaches and other community volunteers. Finally, the parenting coordinator's ability to provide feedback to the court, if necessary, adds to the accountability of the process as coparents learn new coparenting practices.

Children can thrive in shared-custody situations if coparents can work collaboratively and avoid the legal, adversarial process to create an appropriate parenting plan for their situation. Once that plan is established, coparents should choose a model of coparenting that provides adequate child-focused information sharing and functional decision-making. Children's best interests in shared-custody situations are most often served with a parallel parenting model that moves coparents' engagement from face-to-face contact into cyberspace, and when necessary, is supported by the range of coparenting support now available in most communities.

8

Children Need Structure and Routine During a Divorce

Joseph Nowinski

Joseph Nowinski is a clinical psychologist, supervising psychologist at the University of Connecticut Health Center, and author of The Divorced Child: Strengthening Your Family Through the First Three Years of Separation.

During a divorce, structure, predictability, and routine are important to children. They set the stage for the development of social and literacy skills, which divorce can disrupt. Parents can provide such an environment with daily routines. Dinnertime must be scheduled so that parents and children can eat and socialize with each other. In addition, homework time must be designated in the same room so that parents can supervise assignments and children know they can ask for help. Playtime must also be provided; how children entertain themselves must be monitored. Finally, bedtime rituals are necessary for parents and children to reconnect and close out the day.

One theme I have laid out in this book is the idea that, in a child-centered divorce, parents make an effort to minimize severe disruptions in a child's lifestyle and at the same time, that they make an effort to make their child's life predictable and structured. Some people are of the opinion that change itself is necessarily detrimental to children, especially

Joseph Nowinski, *The Divorced Child: Strengthening Your Family Through the First Three Years of Separation*. New York: Palgrave Macmillan, 2010, pp. 129–131. Copyright © 2010 by Joseph Nowinski. Reprinted by permission of Palgrave Macmillan. All Rights Reserved.

the kind of change that separation represents. Yet research suggests that it is not change per se, but rather *unpredictability and chaos*, that are the greater risk factors. Lifestyle change is inevitable for many parents facing divorce, and therefore for their children as well. These include changes in gross income, living accommodations, and disposable income, to name only a few.

The divorcing parent needs to strive not so much to *eliminate* change in their child's life, but rather to *manage* it, and specifically to allow their child to anticipate and plan for such change as much as possible.

Children thrive, developmentally speaking, on routine and predictability. That stability and structure, in turn, sets the stage for them to move forward on the two developmental fronts that are so important at this point in their lives: socialization and literacy. Divorce can be a highly disruptive force. Your goal during these crucial years is to create the kind of environment that will allow your child to stay "on course" developmentally.

> *What you need to do is to insure that your child's life maintains a degree of stability and predictability.*

Daily Routines

One of the most common comments made by parents who are going through a divorce is how much an effect the divorce has had on their daily and weekly routines. "*My life has been turned upside-down*" is a typical remark. Naturally, this means that not only the parent's life has been turned upside-down, but also the child's.

Children's development tends to follow a natural progression. For example, it is fairly well established that all children will learn to talk within a certain span of time, and that they will also learn to read. Little or no formal instruction is needed to learn speech, but some instruction is needed for a child to become literate. Given how complex learning to read is, it is really a wonder how little instruction most children need, and how much progress slower readers can make with even a modicum of extra help.

Structure, predictability, and stability in day-to-day life is as important as instruction is to learning. This is where the disruptive force of a divorce can lead to academic and social deficits that have a long-term effect on a child. To prevent this, you do not have to become your child's tutor or even put in more time on homework than the average parent would. What you need to do is to insure that your child's life maintains a degree of stability and predictability. What follows are guidelines for doing this. If you think of your child's day as one of those old-fashioned pie charts, a good chunk of the pie will be taken up by two activities: school and sleep. Your job as a parent is to make sure that the activities cited below fit into the pie of your child's life on a regular and consistent basis. They should vary as little as possible from day to day, and they should be as predictable as possible. One way for you to accomplish this is to write out a daily schedule and post it somewhere for everyone to see. Let's go through them one by one:

- *Dinner Time*: Perhaps we should not be surprised, given the way our lifestyles have changed, that even two-parent families often struggle to maintain regular mealtimes. Dinner is the most important meal for families. It may be unrealistic to expect either two parents or a single parent these days to reproduce the sort of dinnertime scenario that was depicted, say, by Norman Rockwell in his famous Americana paintings, with everyone seated around the table, napkins in hand, passing around the meat, vegetables, and potatoes. On the other hand, we do not have to totally give in to chaos, with everyone eating separately, in different places and at different times. That kind of situation is not conducive to a child's healthy development. It can limit social development, since the daily family meal is an opportunity for social interaction. Moreover, a chaotic dinner time tends to be a symptom of a larger chaotic family life, which is detrimental to academic success.

- *Homework Time*: Once children start first grade, you can expect them to have some daily homework. Usually this will involve reading, spelling, and basic arithmetic. You may be asked to help your child read a short book, and then sign a check-off sheet indicating that you have done so. Chances are your child will also bring home one or two handouts to be done as homework every day. The best times to assign as homework times are soon after school (following a break for a snack) or shortly after dinner. If you wait too long after dinner you are apt to run into that time when your child's energy and ability to focus is sapped. Do not hesitate to designate a "homework time" and enforce it by turning off all distractions such as television and music. This typically does not have to be longer than twenty minutes to half an hour, depending on what grade your child is in. It is most important that you personally supervise homework. You don't necessarily have to stand over your child's shoulder, but neither should you be in another room occupied with something else. By the same token, although it may make life less stressful for you, do not allow your child to do his or her homework in bed, or with an MP3 player pumping music into his or her ears. Make sure your child knows you are ready and willing to help with homework, and be sure to check your child's homework every day for completeness and accuracy. Finally, don't hesitate to communicate with teachers about any concerns you have about your child's homework.

- *Play Time*: Play time is as important as homework time, but it should also be monitored. During these years your child's play may include: playing video or computer games, either through a videogame console or by visiting an appropriate, child-oriented website (many of which have free games available); watching television; doing puzzles; drawing and other art work; playing with building toys, dolls, or plastic animals; and reading. All of these activities are fine, but your role as a parent is to be sure that your child's play remains somewhat balanced across these various activities. As a rule, children should play computer or video games for no more than one hour at a time. Also, while you do not have to play with your child all the time, you may find some occasional parent-child play time to be a nice break. Finally, as busy as you may be as a single parent, do not allow your child's play (especially if it involves the Internet) to go unsupervised. Play time is best scheduled for right after school and again after homework time in the evening.

- *Bedtime Rituals*: Bedtime rituals are very important to children. They are a means to "close out" the day and reconnect with you. Chances are, you and your child have already established some bedtime rituals. If so, do not let the distraction of divorce allow you to abandon these. Over time these rituals may evolve and change. You can also invent new ones, such as "secret" hand shakes and pledges. During the first three crucial years of your divorce, rituals like the above can play a vital role in helping your child manage any insecurity he or she may be experiencing. That insecurity tends to come out at night—just when bedtime rituals come in handy.

Common elements of bedtime rituals include: reading stories; sharing something interesting or funny that happened that day; saying prayers or meditations; and repeating good-night rituals. If you have more than one child, you may be able to convert some of your bedtime rituals—reading, for example—into something you all do together, to make it a bit more efficient for you. The children's book section in your local library is a good resource for an ongoing supply of age-appropriate bedtime stories.

Whether your current family is large or is just yourself and your child, it is desirable to establish and follow family traditions.

Creating Family Traditions

Take a moment to think back on any traditions your own family may have observed when you were growing up—specially when you were in the same age group as your child is now. Naturally, these memories will be colored by the state of your family at the time. That being said, family traditions are a way of bringing the family together, offer an element of stability and predictability to family life, and are important to cultivate whenever possible.

Most family traditions are built around such things as holidays and birthdays. The following questions are intended as food for thought:

- What traditions did your family celebrate?

- How did your family celebrate these occasions?

- Did you look forward to these traditions?

- How would you have felt if one of these traditions had been cancelled?

63

Whether your current family is large or is just yourself and your child, it is desirable to establish and follow family traditions. For some divorcing parents, the traditions that they had followed before the divorce were centered mostly around their ex-spouse's family. If this has happened to you, it may feel as if you have lost your family traditions. In these cases, it can be helpful to talk to friends about what special family traditions they follow in their own households, and use these ideas as a springboard for developing your own traditions. I encourage divorcing parents to create at least one *new* tradition for their post-divorce family. For example, you can celebrate a holiday you once more or less ignored, or establish a tradition of taking one weekend a year as a mini family vacation.

For instance, one divorcing mother decided to start a tradition on Halloween. She had two children, and at the time of her divorce they were four and six. Since she happened to live in a neighborhood that was conducive to trick-or-treating, in which there were a lot of young children, she decided to start a yearly Halloween tradition of inviting family, friends, and neighbors with children over to her house for pizza and soda. Once all of them had something reasonably healthy in their stomachs, the children went trick-or-treating as a group. The mother's parents volunteered to stay at her home and dole out treats while she and her children were gone. After repeating this tradition two years in a row, this mother's children eagerly looked forward to Halloween.

9

Divorce May Affect How Parents Discipline Their Children

Robert E. Emery

Robert E. Emery is a professor of psychology and director of the Center for Children, Family, and Law at the University of Virginia. He is also author of Renegotiating Family Relationships: Divorce, Child Custody, and Mediation.

Effective discipline, in which parents maintain clear boundaries of authority while expanding their children's autonomy, becomes a problem in divorce. Factors that can affect parents as disciplinarians are guilty feelings, questioning the appropriateness of expectations, and being preoccupied with loving their children. Additionally, children may test the boundaries of authority out of anger or to get attention. For residential parents, difficulties may arise from simply spending more time with their children and dealing with coercive behavior, in which children use guilt to manipulate parents into satisfying their demands. For nonresidential parents, limited time with children may be spent on having fun and "quality time" at the expense of including "down time" and discipline as normal parts of their relationship.

As long as parents respond to the children's needs, not their own, they are not likely to love their children *too* much. And despite their struggles, most parents succeed in

Robert E. Emery, *Renegotiating Family Relationships: Divorce, Child Custody, and Mediation*, 2nd ed. New York: Guilford Press, 2012, pp. 86–88. Copyright © 2012 Guilford Press. All rights reserved. Reproduced with permission.

quickly establishing new boundaries of love with their children. Recall, however, that authoritative parents are loving *and* firm in discipline. Discipline often is a big problem for parents in divorce, at least for a time.

The key to effective discipline is maintaining clear boundaries of parental authority while gradually expanding the boundaries of children's autonomy. Children get to make decisions within their "territory" of autonomy, whether that involves choices about food, clothes, or friends. The key discipline issues are boundary conflicts—for example, dating, driving, and curfews among adolescents.

Unfortunately, guilt, uncertainties about appropriate expectations, or preoccupation with having fun (or otherwise focusing mainly on loving/being loved by children) can make both divorced parents less effective disciplinarians at and well beyond the usual boundaries of parental authority. Perhaps one parent also may have relied on the other to discipline the children, or, when doing the disciplining, at least counted on the other as an ally. Yet, single parents do not have a partner to consult about appropriate discipline, or to enforce rules with them or for them. One parent may find, in fact, that the other is actively undermining their discipline efforts.

Because of their inner uncertainties, parents can mistakenly attribute children's misbehavior to the divorce or related causes, rather than to more normal influences.

As parents struggle with rules, children often behave badly. Sometimes this is due to the distress of divorce. Other times children test the boundaries out of anger, or as a way of seeking attention. Children also may have more selfish motivations; they may just want to get their way. All children "test the limits," particularly during certain developmental stages like the "terrible twos" or early adolescence. Many of children's challenges in divorce are normal, too. The problem, instead, is the parents' discipline, or more accurately, their lack of discipline.

Residential Parents: Learning to Set Limits

Residential parents spend more time with their children, and for this reason if no other, they often encounter more difficulties with discipline. The cliché approach to discipline, "Just wait until your father gets home," conveys a bigger problem that many residential mothers face. Residential mothers (and fathers) sometimes must master an entirely new parenting role.

Other struggles also can make discipline difficult for residential parents. Emotional and practical burdens can lead to a decrease in monitoring of children's activities and misbehavior. Children also may be given increased independence from former family rules, perhaps together with increased responsibilities for helping around the house or caring for younger siblings. Growing up a little faster can have positive consequences, but not all children are capable of adequately exercising autonomy at a younger age.

Parental Guilt and Coercive Interactions

Many problems with discipline stem from parents' guilt and self-doubt. Because of their inner uncertainties, parents can mistakenly attribute children's misbehavior to the divorce or related causes, rather than to more normal influences. Rules that had been standard become a source of internal debate and perhaps an indulgence. Parents now may wonder if it is right to say "No" to bad behavior. They ask themselves if the child is disobeying because they are upset over the divorce. This is a reasonable question, but it generally is one that a parent should ask only *after* enforcing discipline.

Consider the common problem of coercive cycles in interactions between parents and difficult children. In a coercive interaction, children are positively reinforced for misbehavior as parents give in to their escalating demands. Parents, in turn, are negatively reinforced as the child stops pushing once the parent caves in. Since both child and parent are rewarded, the pattern of demand and capitulation continues.

Clarity and consistency are the keys to reestablishing effective discipline in divorce.

In divorce, a unique variation of this common problem occurs when a child learns to pull the guilt trigger. A mother might tell her son that it is time for bed, for example, but the boy pushes for another television show. After two or three ignored warnings, the 8-year-old shouts in anger or in tears, "Dad lets me stay up. I wish I was at his house!" Feeling guilty, or perhaps afraid that her son does not like being with her, the mother caves in, perhaps joining her son to watch another show, or two. As a result of such "successes," children quickly learn to "push the guilt button."

As parents slowly begin to recognize such coercive cycles, they may assume that a child is being malicious—or that the other parent is undermining them. Both problems are possible, but enforcing the bedtime rule still is the appropriate, immediate response. And because testing the limits is completely normal, I often take a few minutes in mediation to warn parents about how to respond. I encourage them to remain consistent, separately and together, in enforcing their usual rules. After all, a child's "job" is to get through life in the easiest way possible. A parent's responsibility is to ensure that the easiest path is the most adaptive one.

Thus, the appropriate focus of renegotiating boundaries of power in parent-child relationships often involves increasing parents' confidence, rather than questioning children's motivations. As with redefining other boundaries, clarity and consistency are the keys to reestablishing effective discipline in divorce. Specific rules are not so important. Bedtime can be 8:30, 9:00, or 9:30. What is essential is having a bedtime and consistently enforcing it.

Nonresidential Parents: Parenting Isn't Always "Fun"

Like residential parents, nonresidential parents also tend to discipline less often and less effectively. In fact, many nonresidential parents discipline their children very little or not at all. These "Disneyland dads" (or "merry-go-round moms") turn their limited time with their children into a trip to fantasyland. Everything is always fun, too much is never enough, and nothing is ever wrong.

Hectic, fulfilled weekends often are motivated by a parent's attempt to make up for lack of quantity time with intense "quality time." Nonresidential parents understandably want to make the most of their limited contact with their children. They may desperately want to have a normal relationship with their children—but fantasyland visits are *not* normal. Normal fathers and mothers do not entertain their children endlessly, and many nonresidential parents need to be reminded of this. A normal relationship includes "down time" and discipline. In mediation, I frequently offer this reality check to parents if things are going badly or to prevent problems from developing.

Not only can children benefit from a more normal relationship with the nonresidential parent, but the relationship between parents also should improve if they both take an active hand in discipline. Many residential parents feel like they do all of the work, while the nonresidential parent has all of the fun. Nonresidential parents who discipline appropriately, however, not only share the load with their coparent but they also achieve their goal of being more of a presence in their children's lives.

10

Adult Children of Divorce Are More Likely to Have Relationship Issues

Geraldine K. Piorkowski

Based in Chicago, Geraldine K. Piorkowski is a psychologist and author of Adult Children of Divorce: Confused Love Seekers *and* Too Close for Comfort: Exploring the Risks of Intimacy.

Adult children of divorce are more likely to get divorced than others. Without having a "blueprint" for a healthy long-term relationship, these individuals may jump from one relationship to another or avoid them altogether. Some adult children of divorce see minor flaws and benign incidences as red flags, magnifying their sensitivities and making them feel unsafe in relationships and wary of love. Others attempt to master what went awry during childhood, choosing partners with the same negative qualities of their parents. Furthermore, the media popularizes the myths of love at first sight and romance as a transformative power, promoting unrealistic standards and expectations. Therefore, adult children of divorce must figure out how their upbringing affected them and create a new roadmap for building relationships in their lives.

Did you grow up with divorced parents? Have you ever given thought as to how that experience may be shaping your own behaviors today?

Geraldine K. Piorkowski, "Confused Love Seekers: Understanding Adult Children of Divorce," *Going Bonkers Magazine*, 4.5, October 2010, pp. 12–13. Republished with permission of ABC-CLIO LLC. Permission conveyed through Copyright Clearance Center, Inc. All rights reserved. Reproduced with permission.

The literature is clear. Adults who grew up in divorced families are twice as likely to get divorced as others, and three times more likely if both partners came from divorced homes.

Especially anxious about romantic love, adult children of divorce either go from one relationship to another or avoid them altogether like the plague. Because they have no blueprint for a long-term, satisfying romantic relationship from their parents, they are understandably confused about what makes a relationship work, and are all too ready to consider divorce when moments of unhappiness strike.

Can't Believe It Will Last

Less trusting of their partners than adults who grew up in intact families, children of divorce are pessimistic about love and quick to see minor flaws as major stumbling blocks. The departure of a parent from the family home often leaves these adults waiting for the other shoe to drop in their own romantic lives. On the lookout for similar trouble, they are wary of love. If their divorced parents fought a great deal, an angry exchange with a partner becomes a red flag signifying trouble ahead.

Adult children of divorce frequently fall in love to make up for the missing ingredients in their childhood.

Similarly, when an adult grew up with emotionally distant parents who later divorced, emotional distance of any kind in a romantic relationship, no matter how temporary or natural, can feel unsafe.

When there was a cheating, unfaithful parent in the picture, mild flirtatiousness or gregariousness on the part of the partner, even when totally innocent, can signal danger in flashing red lights.

Unfortunately, for children of divorce, their parents' problems get dumped in their laps in one form or another. A magnified sensitivity to related problems and skewed interpretations of love are part of that inheritance.

Looking for Love in All the Wrong Places

Adult children of divorce frequently fall in love to make up for the missing ingredients in their childhood. When a strong father figure was absent, women who grew up in divorced families often seek out older, professionally successful men as partners to have someone to love, protect, and care for them. Unfortunately, many of these substitute father figures possess the same negative qualities as their own fathers, e.g. emotional unavailability, alcoholism, or unreliability. Trying to master what went wrong in childhood is part of the motivation, but the similarity to the original parent becomes their undoing. Or these children of divorce are so accustomed to playing a certain role in the family, e.g., that of caretaker, that they look for emotionally immature partners to nurture, just as they did with their mothers or younger siblings. Choosing partners to make up for childhood losses, or to maintain a familiar role, frequently leads to unhappiness because there is very little of substance (in terms of interests and values) to maintain the relationship.

Reaching for the Stars: The Myths of Love

The unrealistic standards for romantic love implicit in TV sitcoms, romantic novels, and movies, set the stage for disillusionment and loss of love. For children of divorce who lacked parental models of a healthy romantic relationship, the media provides an alluring alternative.

TV shows, such as "The Bachelor" with its emphasis on "love at first sight" propose a magical view of love that depends on visceral reaction. Rather than providing guidelines for long-term relationship satisfaction, such TV shows are showcases for infatuation—a short-lived emotion that is based primarily on sex appeal and calls for fantasy and make-believe to survive. In contrast, real romantic love requires (in addition to physical attraction) emotional intimacy or closeness that develops slowly over time as people get to know one another. An additional, desirable component in romantic love is commitment, which is the resolve to make a relationship work well and endure forever, if possible.

Check out which of your beliefs about love are realistic and which ones aren't.

Besides believing in "love at first sight," adult children of divorce tend to believe in the transformative power of love, that is, the notion that love can change frogs and scullery maids into princely creatures. In the modern version of the fairy tale, "the Beauty and the Beast," rogues, drunkards, and other scoundrels become caring and considerate partners once the magic potion of love works its charm. In short, these adults believe that love has the power to change their partners, and themselves, into more ideal people. Unfortunately, the world of love doesn't work that way.

Making Romantic Love Work

Now that you understand the myths of love, and a little more about how being a child of divorce has shaped your own life, it's time to figure out how to make love really work for you.

Recognizing your Hidden Beliefs

Check out which of your beliefs about love are realistic and which ones aren't. Besides the ones already mentioned in the beginning of this article, other dysfunctional beliefs may include:

- unconditional love (she will accept all of your faults, warts and all)

- mind reading (he just knows what you need or want; there is no room for misunderstanding)

- destined or fated love (there is only one person out there for you—your soul mate)

- love conquers all (it doesn't matter how different you are in terms of background, lifestyle, religion, etc., you'll make it work.)

Know What You Want and Why

Identify what qualities you're attracted to, and assess whether it's a positive or negative trait. Also realize that physical attraction (especially the instant kind) is typically based on one characteristic and not the whole person.

Choose Consciously and Wisely

Choose a "best friend" as a romantic partner—someone you can talk to easily about a wide range of topics and who shares your interests and values. Sharing similarities along many dimensions is important. Being able to enjoy the same leisure activities, clubs, and or religious organizations contributes to couple satisfaction. Companionship is an important benefit that gets increasingly valuable as couples get older.

Be Open to Romantic Possibilities in a Wide Range of People

Often sexual attraction follows emotional closeness: it's not necessary to have it the other way around. If you're dating someone regularly for 3–6 months and there's no romantic spark, it's unlikely to develop. Similarly, if you're attracted to someone physically and there's no real emotional intimacy after a period of time, it's time to move on. Some people fall in love slowly over time: sometimes a best friend becomes your lover; sometimes sex is awkward and fumbling at the start; sometimes love is quiet and caring rather than passionate and mind-blowing. In other words, love comes in a variety of shapes and sizes, if you're open to its arrival.

Work Through Your Parents Divorce

Determine how your parents' divorce affected you. What are your sensitivities and vulnerabilities in romantic relationships as a result of the divorce? For example, do you get anxious about being abandoned, betrayed, and/or abused when you get close to someone? If so, your unrealistic fears need to be resolved. Also, blaming only one parent for the divorce is often short-sighted. Most of the time, both parents contributed to the ending of the relationship. Black and white thinking (where one parent is the victim and the other the bad guy) is not helpful in understanding what really went wrong. Also, you need to see yourself as different from your parents, not a carbon copy of either parent or of their life together.

Research has shown that couples who argue in a critical, contemptuous, and defensive manner are more likely to get divorced than those who have disagreements in a warmer, more collaborative, ready-to-compromise style.

Improve Your Skills

Take a course in communication and conflict-resolution skills, which your parents were probably lacking. Research has shown that couples who argue in a critical, contemptuous, and defensive manner are more likely to get divorced than those who have disagreements in a warmer, more collaborative, ready-to-compromise style. Let your partner know what your vulnerabilities and sensitivities are, rather than blame him/her for not being able to fix them.

Create a New Romantic Roadmap

You will require a different roadmap for a long-term, romantic relationship than the one provided by your parents. Find out which of your friends or relatives has a satisfying relationship and interview/observe them to determine how they made it through the rough spots. Read about the "ups and downs" of long-term relationships and how others navigate them. Long-term relationships change over time as fantasy and novelty gradually become replaced by greater emotional closeness.

11

Having Children Can Cause Divorce

Vicki Glembocki

Vicki Glembocki is a writer and author of The Second Nine Months: One Woman Tells the Real Truth About Becoming a Mom.

The number of new parents divorcing and trying to save their marriages is on the rise. Study after study shows what they will not admit: having children does not make marriages happier. In fact, when the first baby arrives, 70 percent of couples experience drops in marital satisfaction. However, parents blame other factors instead, such as work, finances, and the shortcomings of their spouses. Experts state that marriage has changed as an institution since the 1950s; instead of being content with "solid" partners who have defined roles, spouses today expect them to fulfill their every need and help out on every front, which suffers when children are involved. In addition, the timing of these divorces occurs before children grow older and raising them becomes easier.

In June, Melissa* packed the U-Haul with everything that was hers and everything that was theirs—the Disney videos, the Littlest Pet Shop figurines, the ballet tutus, the Dr. Seuss book about the places they'll go.

And she left.

*Names and some identifying characteristics have been changed.

Left the house in Jenkintown she'd been living in for nine years.

Left the man she'd been married to for eight of them, the father of her five- and two-year-old daughters.

Left the life that was nothing like she'd imagined it would be back when having kids was just a hazy someday-down-the-road plan, all "white picket fence and happy, happy, happy," she says.

So she took the girls. And left. For good.

"I'm scared," she says. Will she be able to make it financially on her own? Will the kids hate her for taking them away from their dad? Was this the best decision for them? Or was it simply the best decision for *her*?

Melissa, 36, was certain of only one thing: She couldn't stay married to that man.

Ever since 1979, the divorce rate's actually been dropping.

And she wasn't the only woman she knew who was feeling that way. Of the 10 friends she'd met at the Moms Club she'd joined just after her five-year-old was born, half were now talking divorce. One had already split; one was about to file papers. Two were in last-resort couples' counseling. And one had a five-years-until-divorce plan.

"I feel like I'm surrounded by people with little kids who are trying to get divorced," Melissa says. She wondered if it was just a weird coincidence among her Philadelphia friends, a "divorce cluster." But the more she opened up about what she was going through, the more stories she heard about similar couples all over the country. The news wasn't entirely shocking, given the widely quoted 50 percent divorce rate in this country. Except for one tiny detail: The divorce rate *isn't* 50 percent. Not for Melissa and her friends.

If they'd gotten married in the '70s and were now calling it quits after 35 or so years, they'd be part of the *only* generation ever to hit that 50 percent failure rate—which is where that statistic comes from. But ever since 1979, the divorce rate's actually been dropping, says Wharton economist Betsey Stevenson, who studies marriage and divorce. These days, according to Stevenson, very few people like Melissa—college-educated moms who were in their late 20s when they got hitched—are filing for divorce before they hit their 10-year anniversaries. Their divorce rate? Just *seven percent.*

So why, then, are Philadelphia's marriage therapists seeing more and more new parents on their couches? Why are divorce lawyers hearing more dads and moms debate preschool drop-off in their custody arrangements, rather than college tuition? Why are more kids participating in elementary-school programs implemented to deal with "changing families"? Why are so many parents having affairs, like the one Melissa started when her youngest was only eight months old?

"More of my new parent-clients are saying, 'This isn't good, this isn't for me, I've had it,' and that's it," says Center City divorce attorney Dorothy Phillips.

Study after study now shows that when the first baby comes along, marital satisfaction drops in 70 percent of couples.

This isn't good was exactly what Melissa was feeling. For *her.* She knew her life would be better without her husband and even without her lover, who eventually decided to work it out with his wife. What she didn't know was if it would be better for her two preschool girls. As she unpacked their stuff in their new room that she'd painted wisteria purple, in the two-bedroom condo she bought with help from Obama's rebate, she prayed they'd see it this way: "Mommy is happier than if they stayed together. Why should Mommy stay with Daddy when Mommy's not happy, which makes Daddy miserable because Mommy's not happy? It's living a lie."

Living a Lie

All new parents live a lie, and this is it: *Kids make marriages happier.*

It doesn't matter that parents *want* it to be true, that parenting books and magazines proclaim it to be true, that it's been declared from hospital nurseries near and far for as long as anyone can remember. Back in 1944, a *Better Homes and Gardens* editor put it this way: Once the first child is born, "We don't worry about this couple anymore. There are three in that family now. . . . Perhaps there is not much more needed in a recipe for happiness."

Unfortunately, it's not true. At least, not anymore. Study after study now shows that when the first baby comes along, marital satisfaction drops in 70 percent of couples. While having kids makes moms and dads happier *personally*, it messes up their marriages big-time.

Researchers, though, are really the only ones talking about it. Parents certainly aren't. Who in her right mind is going to casually mention at the next neighborhood block party, "Wow . . . having those kids really screwed up my marriage"? Blaming the kids? Who would admit to *that?*

So they don't. They assume they're the only ones who've connected the timing of starting a family with the onset of marital strife. Instead, they point fingers at acceptable targets—work, finances, spouses not measuring up.

Melissa did just that. Other than doing the dishes, her husband barely helped out after the kids came along. He started to complain about what lots of new dads complain about: They weren't having enough sex; she wasn't paying attention to him anymore. Eventually, they began spending the free time after the kids went to bed doing their own things— she did laundry and made lunches, he messed around in the yard. She felt alone. She went on and off antidepressants, wavering over whether or not she still loved her husband, or if she ever had. When she asked him to go to counseling, he said, "I don't care what you or anyone else has to say. I'm not the one who's changed, it's you."

In a way, it was true.

"I was a scared, meek little person before I had kids," she says. "They made me stronger. They showed me that I had self-worth, that I had an important job to do."

When she went away on a business trip two years ago and, a dozen tequila shots later, ended up in bed with a guy she worked with, she thought it was a one-hit wonder. It wasn't. Her attention turned to secret texts and Facebook chats with a man who himself had a wife and young kids at home. She came up with excuses twice a month to run an errand, telling her husband she needed to pick up a prescription at Walgreens or drop off a letter at the post office, stealing away for a backseat quickie in a parking lot.

Marriage was a different institution [in the 1950s]. Couples expected much less from each other: Mom stayed home and took care of the domestic front, Dad went to the office and took care of the paycheck.

Her husband never found out. Every now and then she'd feel a tinge of guilt—*Why am I doing this to him? Or I should stay with him and be miserable because it's easier*—but by then, there was no marriage left to save.

"I'd been doing it all already," she says. "What did I need him for?"

A Relatively New Idea

Back in the 1950s, she would have needed him. Marriage was a different institution then. Couples expected much less from each other: Mom stayed home and took care of the domestic front, Dad went to the office and took care of the paycheck. Being happy wasn't a requirement; it was a fringe benefit.

"The expectation that marriages should be happy, loving and fulfilling is a relatively new idea," writes Tara Parker-Pope in her new book *For Better: The Science of a Good Marriage.* Today, people are no longer content with marrying "solid" partners who fit into defined roles. Both parents are expected to help out on every front: Mom works, Dad plays Candy Land. Plus, people are waiting to marry until they find fill-their-every-need soulmates. A spouse, then, has to be a provider, and a lover, and a confidant, and a therapist, and a late-into-the-night conversationalist, and a BFF. So when kids come along and so much attention gets filtered to the baby, this you're-my-everything relationship has much more to lose than, say, Melissa's parents' relationship did. Add in that today's parents are part of the Helicopter Generation, feeling societal pressure to be perfect moms and dads who raise perfect kids who make perfect soccer goals and get perfect scores on their SATs. As a result, these parents come home from their demanding, long-hour jobs and obsess over being with the kids every possible second, leaving no time to be with each other.

Is it any wonder, then, that new parents are twice as dissatisfied today as they were in the 1960s and '70s?

"It is very worrisome," says Berkeley's Carolyn Cowan, who, along with her husband Philip, has conducted some of the most influential field research on parenting. "If there's not enough time for parents to replenish their relationship, they get disconnected."

For Erika, 41, in Cherry Hill, "disconnected" was an understatement.

"We were living entirely separate lives," she says. After their twin boys were born five years ago, Erika decided to stay home and do the traditional "mom" role, while her husband took a more stressful, higher-paying sales job to bring home the Pampers. Their setup probably would have worked just fine 50 years ago. Instead, they started keeping score.

"When he came back from a business trip, he owed me a night out with the girls," she says. "If I went to the gym, he got to go to a Phillies game. We should have been doing stuff together. Instead, at night, I ended up watching TV upstairs, and he was watching it downstairs." They had separate interests, separate friends—and no desire to talk to each other about anything other than the kids.

On Facebook, they talk about memories of an easier time, reminisce about when life was a lot more carefree. . . . Instead of working on the marriage, they go to Facebook for validation.

Eventually, he stopped watching TV and started surfing porn on the Internet. She began logging onto Facebook, where she reconnected with an old flame from high school, which relationship counselor Alyson Nerenberg is hearing about during counseling sessions all the time now.

"On Facebook, they talk about memories of an easier time, reminisce about when life was a lot more carefree," says Nerenberg, who practices in Chestnut Hill but sees many Main Line couples who don't want to risk running into their neighbors. "Instead of working on the marriage, they go to Facebook for validation."

After a month of Facebook flirting, Erika came clean.

"So, I'm telling my husband that I have feelings for someone else, and I think he's going to be really upset," she says. "Then he turns around and says he has feelings for someone else too, someone he met at the gym. Neither of us ever consummated those relationships, but even if he had, I wasn't sad. I wasn't pissed. I knew the road we were going down." Her husband knew it, too. They were finally on the same page.

In the same business-like tone of their marriage, they divorced (despite Erika's baffled mom asking her weekly, "How bad is it? He's not beating you. He's not bad to the kids"). They had no arguments over arranging custody, child support or alimony. He still had a key to the house; she had a key to his new apartment. He even waited until she got a job to file papers, so he could keep her on his health plan. The first thing she did when she got her own insurance? Get on birth control.

"I have enough guy friends to 'take care' of me if I need them," she says. "People are very up-front: 'You want to have sex? Okay.' Some are also going through divorces or are already cheating on their spouses. Some appear [on Facebook] to be in perfectly normal marriages and say, 'When I'm in Philly, I'll call you.' But I'm not going there."

When Life Looks Brighter

It was one of the most organized, calculated jobs he'd ever had—hiding his affair from his wife. Mike, 34, would set his cell alarm to ring like a phone in front of her so he could pretend a client was calling, and thus go out and meet his girlfriend. Or he'd tell his wife he had to go to Harrisburg for work, then head off on a plane for a secret trip with his mistress to Atlanta, obsessively checking the weather in central Pennsylvania in case his wife asked when he called to say goodnight. His girlfriend even bought a rope ladder for her second-floor apartment, so he'd have a quick escape on the off chance his wife figured it all out and came knocking.

For the most part, [Mike's] life was exactly how he wanted it to be—he could hang out with a woman he was really in love with while his wife raised his child, and he didn't have to get divorced.

But Mike was pretty sure she wouldn't find out: "Having a kid made my wife brain-dead," he says. Where was the woman, he wondered, who was smart and engaging, the sexy, fun one who could carry on a conversation with anybody about any-thing, not just rattle on about the latest milestone passed by her one-year-old baby girl?

On top of that, becoming a dad was nothing like he ex-pected it would be.

"I had no clue how to interact with a baby. I was surprised I felt that way. I didn't want to be around her," he says. "It was all shocking to me."

So he did anything he could think of to avoid coming home to their Fishtown rowhouse. For the most part, his life was exactly how he wanted it to be—he could hang out with a woman he was really in love with while his wife raised his child, and he didn't have to get divorced, so his wife wouldn't have to go back to work.

Until, of course, that one inevitable mistake, that one day when he forgot to sign out of his Hotmail account on the home computer, exposing two years' worth of romantic e-mails between him and his mistress. At his office, he got the phone call he'd worked so hard to evade: "How could you do this to me?" his wife asked.

The timing couldn't have been worse.

Mike wasn't really sure why, exactly, but he'd started feel-ing differently about the "married with kids" thing. Maybe it had something to do with his wife mulling going back to work, which would have given her more than a three-year-old to talk about. Or maybe it was that three-year-old herself, who was starting to talk and tell stories and develop this delightful personality, which made him now want to be around her all the time. In fact, he'd started cooling things with the girl-friend in order to be home more. "I didn't know if the mar-riage was going to work, but I thought it might be able to," he says. "Suddenly I was thinking, 'This can make sense. I want this.'"

Except it was too late.

By the time divorce attorney Dorothy Phillips sees clients, it usually is.

"More than half of the matters in my office are parents in their 30s and early 40s with young kids, and boy, I did not see that five years ago," she says. She thinks life post-9/11 has something to do with the rise. "People realized, 'You get one bite out of this apple, and I didn't bite it right and I'm outta here.'" Relationship counselor Nerenberg believes Facebook is nurturing an illusion that there's greener grass out there. Center City attorney Randi Rubin thinks that if not for the economy, the number of new parents divorcing would be even higher. Some people "simply can't afford to live separate and apart," she says.

Mike attributes his failed marriage to something much simpler.

"I really wish someone had told me it would get better as the kids got older and started being 'people.' I probably should have known that. But I didn't," he says.

How could he? The fact that satisfaction with marriage drops in almost three-quarters of couples after kids come isn't relayed in parenting magazines. His wife's ob-gyn certainly wasn't passing along those research numbers during the third-trimester ultrasound. There are month-long birthing classes to prepare new parents for one day in their lives, but nothing to prepare them for the days, weeks and months that come after. So *of course* new parents expect to magically experience that 1950s mentality that kids make marriages happier. There's nothing that says otherwise.

And as a result, Mike never heard about those other studies that suggest life starts to look a little brighter when kids hit three years old, and that many marriage troubles start to ebb during the preschool years.

"Somebody should say, 'For the first five years, don't cheat on each other. Do not lie to each other more than you absolutely have to, and just stick it out.' Someone should say that:

'Wait those five years,'" he says. "Because now that I actually *want* to wake up with my kid crawling into bed and *want* to spend Saturday in the park with her, my marriage is over. And there's really nothing I can do about it."

12

Divorce Should Not Be Attributed to Having Children

Michele Zipp

Michele Zipp is a writer and blogger for The Stir, *a parenting website.*

Learning about couples divorcing after having children gives rise to speculation that the kids hurt the marriage. However, divorce should not be blamed on children. If young parents break up, it reveals that the marriage was not strong enough to survive the challenges of being parents. Nonetheless, having children makes divorce far more difficult; parents often believe that they have profoundly let down and hurt their children. Furthermore, parenthood connects couples for life, requiring former spouses to continue interacting with each other long after the divorce.

There are a lot of wonderful things that happen after you get married. Sometimes there's a honeymoon, maybe some nesting, a new kind of closeness, bonding in a different way now that you are hitched. It's usually all beautiful. Just like the months experienced after you have a baby. Sure there is insomnia and moments you are terrified and wonder how in the world are you going to keep this baby alive, but it's all quickly replaced by the wonderment of parenthood and that sweet look on baby's face.

Then you learn about couples having trouble and getting divorced after having a baby. Maybe it's happening to you. It tears the whole first comes love, then comes marriage, then comes baby in a baby carriage fairy tale to shreds. There is pain and hurt and so many whys and why nots and a sadness almost too strong to bear. But it happens. And we learn to deal . . . just like this celebrity couple divorcing just seven months after they welcomed a baby.

The Trophy Wife actress Malin Akerman has been married to Roberto Zincone since 2007. They had a baby this April and Akerman gushed about her son Sebastian and husband saying, "[Motherhood is] amazing, the biggest love you have ever felt in your life. I go to my husband, 'I still love you, just this little one a little more.'" Now, they are getting divorced just months after welcoming a son.

My ex will always be my forever because we had kids together. We are eternally tied, organically, spiritually, through our incredible children.

It's heartbreaking to know these two have ended their relationship. Those words, they just hang there. They once meant so much. Now they are just a reminder of that love that is no longer there. Kind of like the wedding ring. The wedding dress. The wedding album. The photos of the two of you smiling at your kid's birthday. The photos from when you first brought baby home from the hospital. They are all there— these reminders of a love that is no longer there in the same way that it once was. I'm living this now. Learning how to be with my ex and co-parent with him. A new normal forms. Divorce isn't easy—it's harder than marriage.

Not Strong Enough to Survive

So many people have guessed that having kids is one of the reasons my ex and I couldn't make it as a couple. Having kids isn't an easy thing—we have twins who are nearly 4. But I just cannot blame parenthood on my divorce. It's like blaming my children and they are most certainly not responsible. So many couples make it work even after kids—it's a whole different thing, with different responsibilities, but kids don't kill a marriage. If the marriage ends, it clearly wasn't strong enough to survive the ups and downs and all the challenges. And that's why it's so hard to go through divorce when you have children. There are these living reminders of incredible times in your life, when you were happy, when you were excited about the future, when you were thinking about the forever. And divorcing can almost feel like you are letting your children down. The words you hear from others "I feel so sad for the kids" hurt more than you ever thought possible. You feel this deep pain that because your marriage didn't work out, you are hurting your children. No parent wants that.

Divorce, whether you have kids or not, is hard, it's painful, it's so difficult. But the more intertwined you are with your spouse—either by owning a pet together, a home, length of marriage, amount of years together, or having children together—all of that adds so much more to the complexity of the relationship ending. Divorce when you have kids is hard— your ex will always remain in your life, you will see him, have to talk to him about money, perhaps even spend holidays together. And maybe all of that no matter how challenging it can be in the beginning is a good thing. You don't get married only to divorce and never see that person again—that person you thought was your forever. My ex will always be my forever because we had kids together. We are eternally tied, organically, spiritually, through our incredible children. And I'm thankful for that. My marriage wasn't a waste of time—we had amazing times together before and after children. And now, divorced, we will continue to do so as parents. Just in a new way. Getting along is hard sometimes, but worth it. Things that come easy in life are sometimes taken for granted. Hard work gives you strength, perspective, and even happiness. It's not only worth it to get along for the kids, but for yourselves.

13

Some Adolescents Should Have an Influence on Their Parents' Divorce

Michael C. Gottlieb and Jeffrey C. Siegel

Michael C. Gottlieb is a forensic psychologist and clinical profes-sor at the University of Texas Health Science Center. Jeffrey C. Siegel is a forensic and clinical psychologist and has conducted child custody evaluations for three decades.

In divorce arrangements, parents and the courts should give con-sideration to adolescents' preferences in where they want to live and with whom. A teen's ability to make sound decisions and judgments, which is influenced by the kind of parenting received and the brain's maturity, should be evaluated by a mediator or specialist when his or her parents are unable to sufficiently assess his or her needs. In fact, research shows that adolescents' involve-ment is beneficial in divorce arrangements. It reduces conflict by encouraging parents to reach a consensus and provides teens with a greater awareness and sense of control. If they are not in-volved, children risk feeling at the "mercy" of parental actions and decisions during a divorce.

Jim and Joan Jones have decided to divorce. They have two teenagers, Jimmy, 15, and Joanie, 13. Jim and Joan would prefer to settle their differences amicably; but Joan thinks the children would be better off with her, and Jim feels they

Michael C. Gottlieb and Jeffrey C. Siegel, "Should Your Adolescent Have a Say?," *Family Advocate*, vol. 33, no.1, Summer 2010, p. 16. Copyright © 2010 American Bar Associa-tion. All rights reserved. Reproduced with permission.

should be with him. On one hand, they wonder if the children should decide for themselves, and on the other, whether the children's opinions should be sought at all. They decide to ask their lawyers.

When parents of teens choose to divorce, they and the court generally want to consider their teens' preferences regarding where and with whom they will live and how much time they will spend with the other parent. Furthermore, teens want to have their preference known and feel better when their opinions have been considered.

As a result of extensive research on adolescent decision-making, we now know much more about how they think and how capable they are of making such decisions. Following is a primer on what the research shows. It begins with parenting styles.

Authoritarian parents value obedience as a virtue and favor punitive, forceful measures to curb "self-will" at points where the child's actions or beliefs conflict with what the parent thinks is right and proper.

Three Kinds of Parenting

The permissive parent attempts to behave in a nonpunitive, accepting, and affirming manner toward the child's impulses, desires, and actions; consults with the child about decisions and gives explanations for family rules; makes few demands for household responsibility and orderly behavior; allows the child to regulate his or her own activities as much as possible; avoids the exercise of control; and does not encourage the child to obey externally defined standards, which are often considered arbitrary.

Children who are raised in such environments are at risk for disrespecting authority and violating rules. Furthermore, permissive parenting contributes to an increased likelihood of adolescent experimentation with drugs and alcohol, participation in minor delinquency, and disengagement from school. In another study, anxiety and depression were higher among adolescents with parents who reported lower levels of behavioral control.

The authoritarian parent attempts to shape, control, and evaluate the behavior and attitudes of the child in accordance with a predetermined and rigid standard of conduct. Authoritarian parents value obedience as a virtue and favor punitive, forceful measures to curb "self-will" at points where the child's actions or beliefs conflict with what the parent thinks is right and proper. Such parents believe in keeping the child in his or her place, restricting autonomy, assigning household responsibilities to inculcate respect for work, discouraging verbal give-and-take, and believe that the child should accept the parents' word for what is right.

Children who are raised by authoritarian parents may have difficulty establishing their own independence as they have little experience in making decisions for themselves.

The authoritative parent attempts to direct the child's activities, but in a rational, issue-oriented manner. Parents encourage verbal give-and-take, share with a child the reasoning behind the rule or restriction, and solicit objections when the child refuses to conform. Both autonomous self-will and disciplined conformity are valued. Such a parent enforces his or her own adult perspective, but recognizes the child's individual interests and special ways. The authoritative parent affirms the child's present qualities, but also sets standards for future conduct.

Research suggests that these children are most likely to thrive as they are allowed decision making within their capability and appropriately established parental limits.

To be more specific, teens who had either authoritative parents or only a mother who was authoritative reported greater well-being than those with no authoritative parent.

Similarly, fifth graders of parents who exerted greater external control and provided less guidance had poorer academic achievement that year, and within two years, had greater difficulty with self-motivation. In contrast, when parents supported their children's autonomy, the children had higher academic achievement that year and greater internal motivation in seventh grade.

Specific authoritative parenting practices . . . are strongly linked with particular adolescent behaviors, such as better academic achievement, lower drug use, and greater self-reliance.

In a related study, authors found that an authoritative parenting style had a very positive impact on children's self-concept. This study suggests that parents remain an important source of guidance for their developing children, even in late adolescence. Similarly, authoritative parenting provided the most significant contribution to children's ability to cope with adversity, regardless of gender and racial differences.

These studies tell us that parents retain influence in adolescents' lives and may do so even in the face of potentially negative peer influence.

Susceptibility to peer pressure in adolescence increases to a peak around age 14, and declines thereafter across all demographic groups. Resistance to peer influences increases between ages 14 and 18 years of age. Middle adolescence is an especially significant period for the development of a capacity to stand up for what one believes and resist the pressures of one's peers to do otherwise.

Parental Influence Continues

Social scientists had assumed that parental influence is sharply curtailed in adolescence, a time during which peers have greater influence and parents have diminishing control. What we have learned is that parents retain notable, albeit more in-direct, influence over their teenager's peer relations. For ex-ample, specific authoritative parenting practices (e.g., moni-toring, encouragement of achievement, joint decision making) are strongly linked with particular adolescent behaviors, such as better academic achievement, lower drug use, and greater self-reliance. In addition, teens do better and feel better about themselves when they know that their authoritative parents accept them for who they are.

Some adolescents will exhibit more mature decision mak-ing than others. Teens who do should be able to have a greater say in custodial decisions than those who are less capable.

In a related study, parents were more inclined to talk with their teens about their personal or emotional welfare, but they were more inclined to punish when teens misbehaved in areas regarding physical safety and in understanding the rights of others. In response, teens reported feeling that doing nothing was not appropriate for parents when issues regarding under-standing the rights of others and avoiding harm arose. With regard to personal/emotional welfare, teens viewed talking as appropriate, whereas yelling and punishment were not. Teens were more likely to behave in a positive way when they viewed their parents' responses to their behavior as appropriate and reasonable. Therefore, how parents discipline their teens is less important than the degree to which their children view their responses as appropriate.

So what are the Joneses to do? If we look at only these studies, they tell us that if Jim and Joan have been authorita-tive parents, accepting their children as individuals, and disci-plining them appropriately, chances are greater that their chil-dren will make better decision for themselves and benefit from being involved in decision making.

Thinking and Judgment

Adolescents and young adults (generally ages from 13 to 24) take more risks than younger or older individuals, a phenomenon that has puzzled researchers for years. What we've learned is that adolescents' inclination to engage in risky behavior does not appear to be due to irrationality, delusions of invulnerability, or ignorance. Rather, there is a gap in time between puberty, which impels adolescents toward thrill seeking, and the slow maturation of the cognitive control that regulates these impulses. It is this gap that makes adolescence a time of heightened vulnerability for risky behavior.

Recent research on adolescent brain maturation indicates that the systems responsible for logical reasoning and basic information processing (thinking) mature before those responsible for social maturity (judgment). A recent study concluded that it is not wise to make sweeping judgments about the maturity of adolescents relative to adults because the answer depends on the aspects of maturity under consideration. By age 16, adolescents' general thinking abilities are essentially indistinguishable from those of adults, but adolescents' social functioning and decision making, even at age 18, is significantly less mature that that of individuals in their mid-20s.

Widely Ranging Abilities

Socially responsible decision making is significantly more common among young adults than adolescents. This finding challenges the assumption that adolescents and adults are equally competent socially, and, thus, laws and social policies should treat them equally. Instead, the picture is far more complex since adolescents' judgmental abilities range far more widely than we previously had thought. Some adolescents will exhibit more mature decision making than others. Teens who do should be able to have a greater say in custodial decisions than those who are less capable.

This information may place the Joneses in a difficult position if they do not have a clear sense of where their children are developmentally. This is understandable since adolescence is such a moving target. Therefore, Jim and Joan might consider having a child specialist or court-appointed mental health professional talk with the children and provide an initial assessment of their abilities in this regard.

In various studies, teens subjected to more parental hostility than their siblings showed more acting-out behavior, and parental conflict made matters worse. Furthermore, teens who exhibited more behavioral problems than their siblings received more hostile mothering, and, as a result, their younger siblings were also subject to more hostile mothering. Given this situation, when parents divorce, hostile mothering, for example, could easily prompt a teen to want to live with the father, even though such an impulse may not be in the adolescent's best interest.

It is important to understand the complexity of the teen's situation and the bases for his or her preferences within a dynamic family situation.

Along similar lines, marital conflict was associated with lower self-esteem, more acting-out symptoms, and lower academic achievement in children. Children of parents who exerted more psychological control, such as being authoritarian and/or more intrusive, were more likely to be anxious or depressed. On the other hand, parental warmth was associated with children's decreased acting-out behavior and increased self-esteem over time.

If the Jones children speak with a mental health professional, one of the questions that will arise is how have they been reared. Even if it turns out that one or both of them is having some difficulty with their feelings or behavior, this may not be the child's fault. Teens live within the context of a family, and when they have problems, all members of the family should be evaluated to determine the cause of the problem. This assessment should be completed before deciding how much say a child can have. This step is essential since resolving certain family issues may help the adolescent make better decisions for themselves.

One study found that the frequency of parent-child conflict was tied to first-borns' difficulty in transitioning to adolescence, but second-borns experienced no such problems. These findings highlight that all siblings do not have identical problems with their parents as they move into adulthood and that parents may learn from their experiences with older children.

Kids Benefit from Having a Say

Considering teen preferences is difficult because, as noted above, adolescence is a moving target. It is a time of rapid development during which teens experiment and learn about the world as they mature. This period of development brings both opportunities to exercise choice and the consequences of those choices from which parents can often offer little protection. Therefore, understanding how teens make decisions is vital to the discussion. Never uncritically accept what a teen says. Rather, it is important to understand the complexity of the teen's situation and the bases for his or her preferences within a dynamic family situation.

Two Australian articles recently addressed the importance of children's involvement in their parents' divorce. One focused on why children should be heard within the context of mediation when using a child specialist to facilitate the process. One year later, these parents reported a general reduction in conflict and an increase in resolution of subsequent conflicts, and the children agreed. The vast majority of parents stated that their children should have a "say" in where they want to live, but when asked if such preferences should be determinative, only 22 percent of parents felt that it should be, and nearly fifty percent worried that their children might be manipulated in the process.

Seventy percent of all children felt uncomfortable with the process; they wanted to be included, but nearly all said they did not want to have the final say. Children referred to feeling better if they knew what was going on and if they had some control over the situation, rather than being at the "mercy" of their parents' actions and decisions.

The second study made three important points. First, parents who mediated and used a child specialist felt that the feedback they received about their children helped them to reach a consensus on children's needs and to change their behavior toward each other. Second, fathers in this group felt that bringing a child specialist into the process leveled the playing field as it removed mothers from the role of "gate keeper of the truth" about the children. Third, parents' agreements favored stability of residence and improved relationships.

How much say children should have will depend on a number of things, but social science can tell us a good deal. When parents can accurately evaluate their children's needs, they may need little or no decision-making help. But all parents cannot do this, and genuine disagreements may arise. One point that emerges from this research is that if conflict arises, the Joneses would be well-advised to consider hiring a mediator and mental health professional to work out their differences.

Organizations to Contact

The editors have compiled the following list of organizations concerned with the issues debated in this book. The descriptions are derived from materials provided by the organizations. All have publications or information available for interested readers. The list was compiled on the date of publication of the present volume; names, addresses, phone and fax numbers, and e-mail and Internet addresses may change. Be aware that many organizations take several weeks or longer to respond to inquiries, so allow as much time as possible.

Association of Family and Conciliation Courts (AFCC)
6525 Grand Teton Plaza, Madison, WI   53719
(608) 664-3750 • fax: (608) 664-3751
e-mail: afcc@afccnet.org
website: www.afccnet.org

The Association of Family and Conciliation Courts (AFCC) is an international association of judges, lawyers, counselors, custody evaluators, and mediators. The organization maintains a library of videos, pamphlets, and other publications on custody and visitation issues, child support, mediation, and more. AFCC also sponsors parent education programs and conferences on a wide range of child welfare issues.

Child Welfare League of America (CWLA)
1726 M St. NW, Suite 500, Washington, DC   20036
(202) 688-4200 • fax: (202) 833-1689
website: www.cwla.org

Founded in 1920, the Child Welfare League of America (CWLA) is a membership-based child welfare organization. Its primary objective is to make children a national priority by providing direct support to agencies that serve children and families. In addition to sponsoring annual conferences and providing consultation services to child welfare agencies, the organization regularly publishes many different types of materials concerning child welfare issues, including a bimonthly online magazine, *Children's Voice*, and the journal *Child Welfare*.

Children's Rights Council (CRC)
1296 Cronson Blvd., Suite 3086, Crofton, MD   21114
(301) 459-1220
e-mail: info@crckids.org
website: www.crckids.org

The Children's Rights Council (CRC) is a nonprofit organization that serves divorced, never-married families, extended families, and at-risk youth. CRC promotes a society where laws, attitudes, and public opinion affirm the idea that two actively engaged and fully participating parents, regardless of their marital status, provides the best family structure for children. Organized to serve the public purpose of advocating the healthy development of children, it is the mission of CRC to minimize emotional, physical, and economic abuse; the neglect and distress of children; and the development of at-risk behaviors following relationship breakups between parents involved in highly conflicted marital disputes. CRC works to assure a child frequent, meaningful, and continuing contact with two parents and the extended family the child would normally have during a marriage.

Concerned Women for America (CWA)
1015 Fifteenth St. NW, Suite 1100, Washington, DC   20005
(202) 488-7000
website: www.cwfa.org

Concerned Women for America (CWA) is an educational and legal defense foundation that seeks to strengthen the traditional family by employing Christian principles. In addition to providing a collection of the latest research and news concerning the maintenance of the nuclear family, CWA publishes *Family Voice*, a monthly magazine for members, and offers many brochures and pamphlets.

KidsHealth from Nemours
website: http://kidshealth.org

Nemours, established in 1936 by philanthropist Alfred I. du-Pont, is dedicated to improving the health and spirit of children. Nemours also creates high-impact educational projects that positively affect the health of children. These projects are developed through the Nemours Center for Children's Health Media, a division of Nemours completely dedicated to this task. The Center creates award-winning, family-friendly, health information in a number of formats, including print, video, and online. Their KidsHealth website includes sections on coping with parents' divorce.

Kids' Turn
1242 Market St., 2nd Floor, San Francisco, CA   94102
(415) 777-9977 • fax: (415) 386-0959
e-mail: kidsturn@earthlink.net
website: http://kidsturn.org

Kids' Turn is a nonprofit organization that helps children understand and cope with the loss, anger, and fear that often accompany separation or divorce. The organization also helps parents understand what support their children need during this crisis in their lives, so that at-risk behavior by children is averted. Kids' Turn is dedicated to enhancing the lives of these children through improved communication and the knowledge they are not alone. It publishes a blog on the *Huffington Post*.

National Family Resiliency Center (NFRC)
10632 Little Patuxent Pkwy.
2000 Century Plaza, Suite 121, Columbia, MD   21044
(410) 740-9553 • fax: (301) 596-1677
website: www.divorceabc.com

The National Family Resiliency Center (NFRC) provides parents and professionals with programs and resources to help them navigate the emotionally challenging process of separation, divorce, and remarriage. The Center helps children better understand and accept the realities of life-changing experiences in their family, as well as providing the guidance they need in order to identify and express their feelings in a healthy way.

National Youth Rights Association (NYRA)
PO Box 516, Rockville, MD   20848
website: www.youthrights.org

The National Youth Rights Association (NYRA) is a youth-led national nonprofit organization dedicated to fighting for the civil rights and liberties of young people. NYRA has members in all fifty states—over seven thousand in total—and chapters from coast to coast. It offers an online forum on youth rights at home, covering topics such as parental authority and emancipation.

Bibliography

Books

Phyllis Chesler   *Mothers on Trial: The Battle for*
                    Children and Custody. Chicago:
                    Lawrence Hill Books, 2011.

James G. Dwyer   *The Relationship Rights of Children.*
                    New York: Cambridge University
                    Press, 2006.

Carla B. Garrity   *Caught in the Middle: Protecting the*
and Mitchell A.   *Children of High-Conflict Divorce.* San
Baris   Francisco: Jossey-Bass, 2012.

Joseph Goldstein,   *Beyond the Best Interests of the Child.*
Anna Freud, and   New York: Free Press, 1979.
Albert J. Solnit

Elizabeth   *Between Two Worlds: The Inner Lives*
Marquardt   *of Children of Divorce.* New York:
                    Crown Publishers, 2005.

Mary Ann Mason   *The Custody Wars: Why Children Are*
                    Losing the Legal Battle and What We
                    Can Do About It. New York: Basic
                    Books, 1999.

Mary Ann Mason   *From Father's Property to Children's*
                    Rights: The History of Child Custody
                    in the United States. New York:
                    Columbia University Press, 1994.

Christina McGhee   *Parenting Apart: How Separated and*
                    Divorced Parents Can Raise Happy
                    and Secure Kids. New York: Berkley
                    Books, 2010.

David Popenoe   *Families Without Fathers: Fathers,*
                  Marriage, and Children in American
                  Society. New Brunswick, NJ:
                  Transaction Publishers, 2009.

Andrew Root   *The Children of Divorce: The Loss of*
                  Family as the Loss of Being. Grand
                  Rapids, MI: Brazos, 2010.

Philip M. Stahl   *Conducting Child Custody*
                  Evaluations: From Basic to Complex
                  Issues. Thousand Oaks, CA: Sage
                  Publications, 2011.

Trudi Strain   *Surviving Divorce: Teens Talk About*
Trueit   *What Hurts and What Helps.* New
                  York: Franklin Watts, 2007.

Periodicals and Internet Sources

Anonymous   "I'm Better Off Without My Dad,"
                  LA Youth, January–February 2012.
                  www.layouth.com.

Hal Arkowitz and "Is Divorce Bad for Children?,"
Scott O. Lilienfeld *Scientific American*, February 14,
                  2013.

Ruth Bettelheim   "In Whose Best Interests?," *New York*
                  Times, May 19, 2012.

Matt Carver   "Child Custody Considerations on
                  School Grounds," *School*
                  Administrator, August 2011.

Dalton Conley   "Recognizing When Kids Benefit
                  from Their Parents' Divorce,"
                  Atlantic, April 16, 2014.

Cynthia Dizicks   "Divorcing Couple War over Child's
and Kristen Mack Religion," *Chicago Tribune*, February
16, 2010.

Ellen Weber Libby "Is There a Favorite Parent?,"
Psychology Today, March 29, 2010.
www.psychologytoday.com/blog.

Margaret S. Price   "Divorce Issues and the Special
Needs Child," *American Journal of
Family Law*, Spring 2011.

Susan Gregory   "The Divorce Generation," *Wall
Thomas   Street Journal*, July 9, 2011.

Jonathan Weiler   "The (Sometimes) Surprising
and Anne J.   Benefits of Divorce for Parent-Child
Menkens   Relationships," *Huffington Post*, July
11, 2011. www.huffingtonpost.com.

Andrea Whatcott   "Divorce May Be Inevitable, but
Children with Resilient Personalities
Do Well," *Deseret News*, August 20,
2011.

Wisconsin Law   "Commentary: 'Best Interests' Hard
Journal   to Define," July 5, 2010.

Index